PRACTICING

HOSPITALITY

PRACTICING HOSPITALITY

The Joy and Grace of Loving Strangers

Annie McCune

Xulon Press

Xulon Press
555 Winderley Pl, Suite 225
Maitland, FL 32751
407.339.4217
www.xulonpress.com

Unless otherwise indicated, Scripture quotations taken from the Holy Bible, New International Version (NIV). Copyright © 1973, 1978, 1984, 2011 by Biblica, Inc.™. Used by permission. All rights reserved.
Scripture quotations taken from the King James Version (KJV) – public domain.
Scripture quotations taken from the New King James Version (NKJV). Copyright © 1982 by Thomas Nelson, Inc. Used by permission. All rights reserved.
Scripture quotations taken from The Voice Bible (VB) Copyright © 2012 Thomas Nelson, Inc. The Voice™ translation © 2012 Ecclesia Bible Society All rights reserved.
Scripture quotations taken from the English Standard Version (ESV). Copyright © 2001 by Crossway, a publishing ministry of Good News Publishers. Used by permission. All rights reserved.
Scripture quotations taken from The Message (MSG). Copyright © 1993, 1994, 1995, 1996, 2000, 2001, 2002. Used by permission of NavPress Publishing Group. Used by permission. All rights reserved.
Scripture quotations taken from the Holy Bible, New Living Translation (NLT). Copyright ©1996, 2004, 2007 by Tyndale House Foundation. Used by permission of Tyndale House Publishers, Inc.

Paperback ISBN-13: 978-1-66289-051-2
Ebook ISBN-13: 978-1-66289-052-9

Endorsements

"Having been a guest in Annie's home many times, I can testify to her unique and beautiful gift of hospitality. In this wonderful book, Annie reveals that hospitality is not merely a gift given to a faithful few, but it is a commandment given by Jesus when he said, "If you love me, feed my sheep." Her captivating personal stories inspired and motivated me to think longer and harder about how I am "feeding the sheep" in my own sphere of influence. We may not all be able to do what Annie has done, but we can all do better."

~**Gina Detwiler**, author of *The Ultimate Bible Character Guide, The Forlorn Series*

"Extraordinary...fresh...heartwarming...and deeply convicting! Annie offers us a rare and transparent glimpse into a life yielded to the radical love of God through the often overlooked, but powerful transformative gift of "hospitality"! You will laugh and cry while your heart is inspired and refired!"

~**Pastor Gabrielle Beam**, Urban Gospel Movement Visionary & Convener, and International Prayer Leader

"Annie McCune has given remarkable leadership to prayer movements these past years. Her winsome ability to engage others is evidenced by her authorship of this important book on hospitality."

~**Mac Pier**, Founder, Movement.org; Lausanne Co-Catalyst for Cities

"What a powerful story is told in Annie's book. Simple welcomes become great adventures. Real emotions and honest fears result in great blessing. I am inspired by how we can change the world by opening our doors!"

~**Vicki Jefferis**, Co-founder Teen Challenge Haiti

Dedication

I dedicate this book to my children: David, Mary Beth, Christopher, and Mark. You are the special agents of God's grace that made each stranger in our house feel deeply loved and accepted.

For my grandchildren: Hannah, James, Harper, Molly, Theo, Isabel, Matti, Garrett, Bernadette, Cory, Audrey, and Rocky (Raquel): May you find joy and grace as you continue to practice hospitality in the generations to come.

Acknowledgments

first want to acknowledge Jesus Christ as my Lord and Savior. He loved me even when I was distant. He invited me to come close and loved me like no other. He calls me a friend. His hospitality has meant everything to me.

I want to thank my amazing husband Lee who has partnered with me in loving hosts of strangers for over 4 decades. He has also been a great support to me as I endeavored to find the time and courage to write these stories down.

I want to thank my many friends who have welcomed me, encouraged me, prayed with me, and inspired me to continue practicing hospitality and writing.

I also want to thank my original Vogt, Koessler, and McCune families, and my "bonus" family members from around the world, who continue to teach me so much about loving strangers as family.

Please note, some of the names and places have been altered in this book for the protection of others.

Table of Contents

"Hospitality is not to change people,
but to offer them space where change can take place."
- Unknown[1]

---

[1]   Goodreads.com

Chapter I

Loving Strangers

Philoxenia: Love the Stranger as Family

The Saturday before Labor Day in 2022, we arrived in Atlanta by car, leaving our home of 32 years in Orchard Park, NY. We attended church on Sunday where they announced community groups would be forming at 5 p.m. Knowing how important it would be for me to make new connections since my husband Lee was not going to move for several weeks due to work obligations, I signed us up online to join a group.

We returned to the church at five p.m. and found our way to where several couples were sitting around the sign "Group 7." Only a few people seemed to know each other. My husband and I took tentative seats around the circle of chairs and smiled timidly at the others. One of the group members had been instructed to be the leader for the night.

We were to briefly introduce ourselves, and then determine a leader for the next meeting, find a home to meet at, and assign someone else to bring a snack. The first official meeting was to be on Wednesday of that week.

We introduced ourselves around the circle sharing information on how long we had been attending the church (24 hours for us), if we were single or married, how many had kids, etc. Then came the time to determine how things would run for the next meeting. One man quickly offered to lead the group and another couple quickly offered to bring snacks. Next came the question of where to meet. The couples and singles who had not volunteered for the other two tasks began one by one to explain why they couldn't host. One woman was undergoing surgery that week, another's spouse was going to be out of town. All had good reasons.

When they looked at Lee and me, I laughingly stated they were welcome to come to our house, but they might have to sit on boxes since the house was currently empty. Our moving trucks were scheduled to come on Monday.

The leader of the group nodded and said, "That sounds great! We will see you at your house Wednesday at seven-fifteen."

The furniture did arrive on Monday, and Lee and I spent Tuesday and Wednesday morning frantically taking things out of boxes and trying to make the family room of our new house feel like a home. Wednesday at 7:15 p.m. we welcomed our new Community group into our home. It was a bit surreal and miraculous, to see fifteen strangers come and begin to relax together. Most of us had not known each other longer than the hour we had spent on Sunday in the "awkward circle." By the end of this first meeting, someone suggested that instead of moving from house to house, perhaps the group could continue to meet in our home. Apparently, we had done enough unpacking to make it feel like a home.

One week in the fall, both Lee and I were going to be out of town so I asked the group if they would want to meet somewhere else that week. When no one responded, I told them they were welcome to meet at our house if someone was willing to let me show them how to open our home and serve as host. A hand flew up and I had the opportunity to meet one-on-one with a new friend. We shared a special time of fellowship as I showed her the door codes and where I kept the coffee and tea. The group met that week and every week at our home until the community groups took a break for the summer.

On a few occasions, we had obligations away from the house on Wednesdays and realized we were going to be late for our own meeting. It was comforting to know the group knew how to get in on their own, and it was fun to have them greet us when we finally arrived! Strangers were becoming friends. Grace was present. We were all very aware something special was happening in our shared space.

These gatherings that began meeting in our new home only days after our move to a new state caused me to reflect on our experiences of hospitality over many years. Lee and I have a continual sense of joy that we have had a place to share and the freedom to do so. From the beginning of our marriage, God taught us whatever roof we happen to be living under, the house does not belong to us. It is His. We are stewards entrusted with what He can use as a sacred space. The spaces we are given are for family, friends, and strangers to gather and be refreshed. Hospitality is usually about being present with our guests, but I have also found when I prepare places for others, God shows up in those spaces even when I can't be there physically.

One thing I need to make clear here at the beginning is the kind of hospitality I am describing is not synonymous with entertaining. Entertaining is about providing someone with amusement and enjoyment. Hospitality goes much deeper. At its core, hospitality is about loving strangers. Several places in scripture encourage us to "practice hospitality."

The two Greek words for hospitality used in the New Testament are *philoxenos* and *philoxenia*. Both mean loving strangers as family members. This is easy to understand at face value, but almost impossible to implement without God's help. It assumes we love our family members. We are usually given an innate sense of love for family. But loving strangers in the same way? No wonder we need to practice!

Perhaps, you live in an area where you are fearful or hesitant to open your door to strangers. Perhaps you don't feel ready to let people into your space or share your food with people you were not planning to feed. Perhaps, looking people in the eye is difficult for you.

Though I know all those feelings, I also know I serve a God who embodies hospitality. He created us all in His image. Therefore, I continue to overcome my fears by trusting He will give me the grace to pursue this practice.

What does it mean to "practice" loving strangers as family? Do I "practice to make perfect," "practice" when I feel like it, or make it a daily "practice" and an integral part of my lifestyle? The latter is what God is hoping for me and I believe it encompasses my personal living space and extends to my workplace, school, church, parks, and grocery store. It can be about sharing meals, or can be as simple as smiling at people throughout my day. Loving strangers (and family, friends, and acquaintances) can be easy, and it can be hard.

Jesus invited His disciples to follow Him, to eat with Him, and to spend time in His presence. He often depended on others to open their homes so those meetings and meals could occur. He practiced hospitality in the most perfect way: with a genuine and sincere love for strangers. He chose to love all of us when we were strangers to Him. His instruction to His disciples on the night before He died was that His followers would bear fruit by obeying His command to "Love one another." He prayed to His Father, "May they be brought to complete unity. Then the world will know that you sent me and have loved them even as you have loved me" (John 17:23 NIV). The Gospel is best spread in the context of love on display. Often, this display of love starts with hospitality.

The practice of hospitality is about learning to love strangers with God's help and grace. It concerns me that one of the reasons our communities and our churches are not thriving these days is because we have forgotten how to love strangers. God has given us all the ability to show hospitality in some way. We don't need to know how to cook or set a table. We do need to overcome our fears. I know I need more practice. How about you?

Throughout the course of my life, I have had the privilege of loving many strangers through opening the door to my home and my heart. In return, I have been radically loved when I was a stranger in need of hospitality. Each experience and relationship have changed me in some way for the better. Those experiences continue to fuel my desire to extend true hospitality to others. This book shares some of those marvelous stories. Sharing how those stories have led me to understand God and some biblical scriptures reflecting hospitality in beautiful and deeper ways are also included. Will you join me on this journey of learning how to practice hospitality the way God intended us to? It will be an adventure full of joy and grace.

> *When I took the risk of opening my new home to strangers,*
> *I never could have imagined how much*
> *I would grow to love each one of them in*

> *such a short time. No one remains a stranger for long when we reach out to them in love.*

Note: At the end of each chapter there are questions to get you thinking about your own understanding and experience of hospitality. There is also a "Dig Deeper" section for those of you who may want to study some of the biblical passages in greater depth. You can always come back to them later.

Ask Yourself...

How did I feel when I was the new person in a group, neighborhood, or church?

_____

_____

How did I feel when no one invited me to their group, home, or pew?

_____

_____

How did I feel when someone invited me to their group, home, or pew?

_____

_____

Have I welcomed any strangers this week? If not, what kept me from it?

_____

_____

How has this chapter challenged me to be more hospitable to strangers?

_____

_____

Dig Deeper...

Read the following Bible verses and record what impacts you concerning God's perspective on hospitality, especially to strangers.

Romans 12:13.

———————————————————————————

———————————————————————————

Hebrews 13:2

———————————————————————————

———————————————————————————

"The kiss of the sun for pardon,
the song of the birds for mirth,
One is nearer God's Heart in a garden
than anywhere else on earth."
- Dorothy France Gurney[2]

---

[2]   Pinterest.com

CHAPTER 2

Hospitality and the Garden Party

In the beginning, God invited a young couple to come into His garden and get to know Him better. Spoiler alert: They proved to be terrible guests!

Hospitality Begins in the Garden

Have you ever been to a beautiful garden created by people you didn't know well? There is something irresistibly lovely as you take in the amazing colors, shapes, scents, and textures of flowers, trees, grasses, paths, and water features that have sprung from the imagination of one person, and often are executed by teams of talented and hardworking people over many years.

While Lee was doing his residency in Family Practice at Lancaster General Hospital in Lancaster, PA, we discovered such a garden. It was a magnificent place called Longwood Gardens in Kennett Square, PA.

We were a young couple without children, and on our days off, we would drive to the gardens to be refreshed. We were mesmerized by our walks through these gardens and delighted by the fountains and indoor and outdoor displays. We learned there was an opportunity to experience the gardens in an even more personal way. In the spring, after the gardens were closed to the public, but while the days were getting longer and warmer, we were invited to bring bikes and ride through the gardens until sunset. The azaleas and rhododendrons were in full bloom. It was magical. Often, we would ride through the paths and woodlands and not see another soul. It felt like the gardens had been created just for the two of us, and God had set this array of beauty just for us to see and experience in the cool of the day. We were so grateful to those who had designed the gardens and tended them for us to enjoy.

Gardens are for sharing. There may be truth to the quote from Dorothy France Gurney mentioned at the beginning of the chapter. Whether or not you are nearer God's heart in a garden I cannot prove, but I do know there is not a garden in the world where God is not present. All gardens and everything in them have come from the imagination of our Creator God. The origin of every plant we see today, no matter how hybridized now, originated in

His mind and heart without human intervention. Gardens have long been a key ingredient for Him to provide us with a hospitable place to dwell. This brings me back to Genesis, the first garden, and the first origins of hospitality.

When God created Eden, His intention was not for His own enjoyment alone. He created it with the purpose of sharing it with us. His love for Adam and Eve included giving them the responsibility of tending His beautiful garden. Genesis 3:8 says in "the cool of the day," as the sun was setting and the evening breezes began to blow, God would meet with them to walk and talk. Adam and Eve would arrive at the end of each day in all their weariness, and vulnerability, and be invited into His full Presence.

As a loving host, God welcomed them by day and walked with them night after night. He gave Adam and Eve permission to touch and taste every tree and plant in the garden except one. His hospitality, gracious in every way, also included some set boundaries. In the story we all know, His guests, Adam and Eve, allowed their curiosity, pride, and humanness to overcome their knowledge and respect for the "house rules." They broke them. The rest of Genesis 3 tells the tragic story of what happened when they overstepped the boundaries God had set for their own good and they were eventually banned from the Garden of Eden.

Fortunately, this is not the end of God's story of hospitality towards them or us. One of the beautiful lessons is that an essential part of biblical hospitality is not so much dependent on a place, as it is on the presence of the host. God continued to be present in the lives of His guests even when they had to figure out how to make their own gardens.

For me, a lesson from this story is the vivid reminder there may be a cost as we practice hospitality. Our guests may touch things we ask them not to touch. There may be a guest or two who overstep our house rules in other damaging ways. The material "stuff" of our lives may take a beating. However badly our guests behave, it will probably never compare to the damage done by the sins of Adam and Eve. It's important to maintain a spirit of grace and forgiveness.

God has provided His Spirit to help us. Stuff can be replaced. It's our work to focus on loving strangers and trying to repair the relationship as far as it concerns us. Let's make sure we don't allow the possibility of an unruly guest to dissuade us from applying ourselves to this important gift of hospitality and receiving all we might gain in return.

Hospitality is always worth the cost in the end.

As I read Scripture, I see a thread of hospitality being woven throughout the whole sixty-six books of the Bible and the history of God and His people. The thread starts in the first book, Genesis, with an invitation to the Garden. The thread continues through the last book, Revelation, where God prepares a new place with space for all of us, and then invites us to a wedding feast. God did not give up on practicing hospitality and neither should we. When I read Scripture through a lens of hospitality, I see how vital this practice is to the story of God's heart for all people and His kingdom advancing.

> **If we desire to be God's hands and feet, we must embrace the spirit of hospitality, despite the potential of unruly guests.**

Ask Yourself...

Have I ever felt God's presence in a garden either I or somebody else planted?

_____

_____

What are my thoughts on setting boundaries for guests in my home or garden?

_____

_____

Have I ever broken something in someone else's home? What was their reaction?

_____

_____

Has any guest broken something in my home? What was my reaction?

_____

_____

Dig Deeper...

Read Genesis 1-3.

Do you see a thread of Hospitality anywhere in these verses?

_____

_____

Is hospitality about the place, or the presence of the host?

_____

_____

"What makes the desert beautiful," said the little prince,
"is that it hides, somewhere, a well."
- Antoine de Saint-Exupéry, *The Little Prince*[3]

CHAPTER 3

Hospitality in the Desert

"In a desert land He found him, in a barren and howling waste. He shielded him and cared for him; he guarded him as the apple of his eye." (Deuteronomy 32:10 ESV)

M uch of the area outside of Eden was wilderness and desert: difficult to cultivate and navigate. Adam and Eve and their descendants learned new ways to survive and help others do the same. Especially in the wilderness areas, travelers who were not deemed threats were extended hospitality to ensure their protection and survival. This practice continues to this day, especially in the arid desert regions of the Middle East.

> *"The Bedouin nomads, Arabic for 'Desert People,' are considered as 'Ideal Arabs' within the Arab community, due to their pure lifestyle of constantly moving and their society and more importantly: their extraordinary Arabic hospitality, which is the core of modern Middle Eastern hospitality.*
>
> *The correct term to describe Arabic hospitality (and generosity) is 'Karam'. Karam is very important in Middle Eastern society, it has shaped the way of living in the Middle East."*[4]

Lee and I experienced this type of hospitality on a trip through Israel. We were part of a study group led by Ray Vander Laan in the fall of 2000. We trekked over 90 miles in fourteen days following our leader. Ray believed in teaching us the way he imagined Jesus taught His disciples. It was common practice in those days for Rabbis to have students who would follow them and learn from them.

For Jesus' disciples, no syllabus or class schedule was provided. They learned as they followed their rabbi day by day. This was basically true for us on our trip. We were given a loose itinerary, but no real idea of where we were going or what lessons we were to learn on any particular day.

For our first several days in Israel, we spent most of the time in the desert visiting places where Abraham and the

---

[4] https://placement-international.com/blog/
karam-the-ancient-art-of-middle-eastern-hospitality

Israelites had lived. We hardly saw any other humans until we returned to the kibbutz at night.

Each day, our "rabbi" Ray would have the tour bus drop us off at a remote location and give the command, "Follow me!" He would tell us whether this was going to be a "one water bottle hike" or "two and bring an extra between two of you." About four days into our journey in Israel, the command for "two and an extra" was given as we debarked in a remote desert setting. It was about noon. It was hot and dry, and the temperature was already climbing well into the 90s.

We followed Ray onto a sandy road seemingly headed nowhere, surrounded by high hills of sand. No vehicles took this road, although we occasionally spotted a few camels and their riders crossing up ahead. We walked on following our leader through this "dry and weary land where there was no water" (Psalm 63:1 ESV). We had brought our own, but it was running out. We knew better than to complain or ask too many questions. We looked around trying to understand what Ray was trying to teach us.

We were about to learn an important lesson about desert hospitality. A runner had gone on ahead to let a nomadic Bedouin tribe living in the area know a group of forty-five American tourists were hiking through and about to pass by their encampment.

When we arrived at the semi-circle of large and small tents, the women and children came out of their tents to greet us. They knew we would be hot, tired, thirsty, and in

21

need of hospitality. They had small cups of water and tea for each of us. They invited us to sit down in one of the larger tents where the sides were drawn up and the breeze was blowing through. Then, as we watched, they lit a fire in a small pit and oiled up their large inverted bowl-like pans.

Some of the women were kneading bread and threw these huge rounds of dough over the upside-down pans. Soon the smell of fresh baked bread filled the air, making our stomachs growl. The women took the large thin pan-cakes of steaming bread and passed them on to us. We were invited to break off a piece of the bread and dip the ends into a bag of dried spices which they also passed around from person to person.

We broke bread together, literally; the hot, sweaty, Christian American tourists foolish enough to hike into the desert at high noon, and the gracious hospitable Arab Israelis. We chatted through an interpreter and spoke to those who knew some English. Ray, who I imagine had been to see this family before, encouraged the women to show us some of their sewing projects and beautifully hand-stitched embroidery.

We felt like we had been invited into their world in a personal way. Then, in an unusual act of Karam (generous giving) and hospitality, we were invited to come into the sheik's special tent for coffee. Customarily, only men were allowed to sit down there. On this occasion, he invited all of us, men and women alike. Ray sat next to the head of the tribe at the front of the tent and spoke to him while we sat facing them, and tried to take it all in. When the sheik offered to kill a goat for us to share in an evening meal, Ray graciously declined on our behalf. After a time of proper thanks and conversation, our rabbi eventually led us back into the desert the way we had come now that the heat of the day had passed.

The more I pondered this amazing experience of *philoxenia,* stranger-loving hospitality, the more I realized how much I could learn from it. An important key to the desert hospitality we were offered by this Bedouin tribe was their readiness to expect unexpected guests (or dozens of guests in our case). It expanded my understanding of control as a host and graciousness as a guest. Hospitality is not about knowing the guests you have invited will come at a certain time and being upset if they come early or late. A lifestyle of hospitality means you are ready to offer shelter and provision to whoever may need it, whenever they need it.

It requires more constant readiness on my part, and trusting more tangibly in the God who provides, for both host and guest, whether those guests are family, friends, or strangers. When we arrived, the women who made bread for us did not have several extra loaves ready. They made them once they recognized our needs. Would I be ready to offer hospitality as graciously if a busload of sweaty, hungry, and thirsty, strangers showed up at my door unexpectedly?

Abraham Welcomed Strangers

There is a story of desert hospitality found in Genesis 18. Abraham looked up from inside his tent and saw three men standing under one of his trees seeking some shade from the hot sun. Abraham hurried out to greet them and asked permission to humbly serve them by bringing them water, washing their feet, and giving them a place to rest. He then asked Sarah to quickly make them some bread. He commanded a servant to prepare a calf. (Sounds familiar, doesn't it?) He brought the guests curds and milk from the calf before serving them the meat.

The three guests, traditionally recognized in Christian theology as God the Father, God the Son, and God the Spirit, accepted the meal under Abraham's tree and then prophesied a blessing over Abraham and his wife. They announced that when they returned the next year, Sarah would bear a son named Isaac.

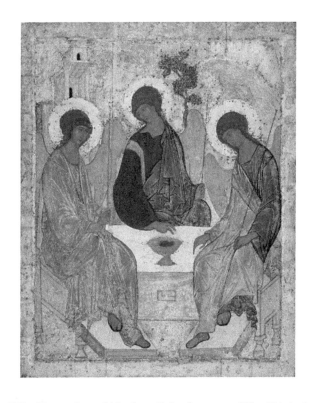

"The Hospitality of Abraham," also known as "The Trinity"

By 15th-century Russian artist Andrei Rublev (Public domain)

Russian artist Andrei Rublev painted a depiction of this scene of hospitality in the 15th century. In it, we see the three figures sitting at the table and a square door in the front center of it. This is meant to represent the open invitation for us to come to the table as well. The Lord was gracious to Sarah and brought laughter and a child named Isaac (which means laughter) into their home and legacy.

> *Hospitality can result in laughter and an increase in blessings for all of us.*

Busloads of Strangers

Ironically, several years after our Israel trip, Lee and I had two opportunities to invite busloads of strangers into our home. The first bus was loaded with a group of environmentally-minded Ultimate Frisbee players from Dartmouth College. They were driving from Hanover, New Hampshire to Seattle, Washington in a repurposed old school bus fueled on used vegetable oil from fast food restaurants. We were the first stop on their itinerary. They parked the bus in front of our house and out tumbled about fifteen sweaty, hungry, thirsty college students who began throwing frisbees and running all over our yard.

Our neighbors came out and wanted to know how long the bus and visitors were planning on staying. They weren't as excited as we were to have these strangers honor us with their visit. It was only one night, but it was joyous and memorable. We were able to engage with the students, learn from them, feed them, and give them a good night's rest before they set out again on their journey across the States and Canada. At each stop, they taught about fossil fuels and gave demonstrations in ultimate frisbee. We were able to offer sincere hospitality to a group of students, most of whom had been strangers, and many of whom we kept in contact with for years afterward.

Unfortunately for them, their bus broke down a few weeks after leaving us. They were stranded for four days in Moose Jaw, Saskatchewan while waiting for parts to fix the bus. At that point in their journey, they could have used some *karam* from Bedouins or Christians to take them in and show them loving hospitality. It did not happen. They did finally make it to the frisbee tournament in Seattle, and back to New Hampshire several weeks later, quite exhausted from the road trip. They are all amazing at catching frisbees and I hope they also caught the importance of hospitality.

The second story involved a bus carrying Ballet Magnificat, a professional ballet company based in Jackson, Mississippi. Each year, their premiere dancers tour the U.S. and select cities around the world. In October 2006, the troupe came to our town in Western NY to perform. One of the ways they were able to charge so little for their excellent productions was to ask churches in the areas where they performed to host the members of the troupe. This included the founders, Keith and Kathy Thibodoux.

Kathy is an award-winning ballerina who danced professionally for many years. Keith's credits include the roles of Little Ricky on the *I Love Lucy Show* and Johnny Paul Jason on the *Andy Griffith Show,* and playing drums for a group of touring musicians called *David and the Giants.* They arrived in Western NY on a cool but colorful mid-October afternoon. We had agreed to host four of the dancers, so we picked them up, fed them, and got them back to the church in time for the performance.

The weather changed quickly while we watched the show, and we came outside surprised to see about 3 inches of light snow already on our car. This was a bit early for snow and we laughed, brushed it off, and drove the dancers to our home. None of them had come prepared for winter. They were used to the warm autumns in Mississippi and had jackets but certainly no mittens, hats, or boots!

Little did any of us expect that by 5 a.m. the next morning, over 2 feet of wet snow would have fallen on our town. The heavy wet snow pulled down tree limbs which had not yet lost their leaves. Thousands of homes lost power which for some would not be restored for 2 weeks. The bus which Ballet Magnificat had driven was stuck in the church parking lot with tires covered in ice and snow. The main highways were all closed. There was no way they would be able to make their next performance in Rochester, NY.

We started getting phone calls from our church asking, "Did we have power?" Strangely enough, we did, though most of our neighborhood was without it. "Could we house a few more?" It turned out ours was one of the few homes in WNY with power and the only one of the host homes with power and heat. Within a few hours, our house was filled with sixteen dancers and Keith and Kathy.

One of the things I have learned in years of opening my door is God often sends me more people than I am comfortable accommodating. No matter how big the house, He always stretches my self-imposed limits, sends a few more, and then astounds me with His supernatural provision! Something I should have learned from my desert lesson.

While we scrambled to find food and warm clothes for the large group, other neighbors came over to help cook and brought blankets and pillows. The dancers had a blast. Many had never seen snow. We found enough boots, coats, hats, and mittens so they were able to rotate, and everyone who wanted to play outside got to experience "lake effect" snow in WNY. Most did not stay outside for long!

In the afternoon, I got a call from the father of a friend of our youngest son. This man happened to be an *I Love Lucy* fanatic. He had learned through the grapevine Little Ricky was staying with us.

"It's not fair," he said. "You don't even care that he is famous!"

He wanted to know if he could come over once the roads cleared. Keith was excited to meet a fan of his and the Lucy show. The house continued to fill up with unexpected strangers. We pulled up chairs and put out more food. What I remember most was sitting at the kitchen table learning from each other and laughing together. Hospitality is a great way to make a snowy October crisis pass all too quickly. The next day, the snow melted enough to dig out the bus and get it back on the road. Ballet Magnificat returned to Mississippi. We washed lots of dishes, bedding, and towels, dried out lots of winter gear, and returned borrowed things to neighbors. Almost twenty years later, I still delight in remembering the joy we had in hosting our expected and unexpected guests, and I would do it again in a heartbeat.

So far, no other busloads have shown up at our door, but I try to be ready to welcome them whether I am fully expecting them or not.

Ask Yourself...

What would I do if a group of unexpected people showed up at my door or in my neighborhood?

_____

_____

Weather disasters happen all over. When they do, am I more concerned for my own survival or others?

_____

_____

Have I ever thought about seeing if there is someone who may need my help?

_____

_____

After reading this chapter, how am I going to prepare to offer hospitality to unexpected guests?

_____

_____

Dig Deeper...

Read Scripture through a lens of hospitality and see how vital this practice is to the story of God's heart for all people and His kingdom advancing.

Record what you discover.

_____

_____

_____

_____

_____

_____

_____

_____

_____

_____

_____

_____

_____

"The word *hospitality* in the New Testament comes from
two Greek words.
The first word means *love* and
the second word means *strangers*.
It's a word that means love of strangers."
-Nancy Leigh DeMoss[5]

---

[5] AZQUOTES.com

CHAPTER 4

Hitchhikers and
Wedding Crashers

During my college years, I was the recipient of extraordinary experiences of hospitality. One of the most unusual happened while studying abroad in Bourges, France in 1977.

It was near the end of our ten-week term when my professor announced a surprise homework assignment for the weekend. She passed around a bowl with folded papers. Each paper had the name of a small town surrounding Bourges. We were told to find the student or students whose town matched ours and form groups around the room.

Then came the assignment: take no money, and hitchhike to the village you have chosen. Research the town and use your foreign language skills to talk your way into someone's home for the night. Then, hitchhike back the next day and meet up with the class on Monday to compare adventures. There were some laughs and looks of incredulity until we realized she was serious. We had read about a similar adventure in one of the textbooks by the famous language professor John Rassias, whose goal in teaching language was to make it real, necessary, and fun.

Matched with a quiet classmate named Bob, whom I did not know well, we were to travel to a town called Henrichemont about thirty miles from the city. As a new Christian, I felt the awkwardness of this requirement for a good grade. Would it be safe? Appropriate? Yet, I felt a peace about going, and that God would protect me. We agreed to meet the next morning near the home where he was staying on a main road. We laughed when we discovered neither of us had hitchhiked before and we had both brought some money "just in case."

Feeling a little more at ease, Bob stuck out his thumb and in what seemed like less than a minute, a small red car driven by a young couple pulled up alongside us. They rolled down the window and asked where were going.

"Henrichemont," we told them.

They looked at each other, shrugged, and said, "Hop in, we will take you there."

They were a newly engaged pair and were out for a weekend drive. Henrichemont sounded great to them. They dropped us in the center of the little town and drove off. Bob and I went directly to the only hotel in town and asked if they had two rooms.

"No, we are fully booked," they replied.

We realized we might have to fulfill the assignment the way our professor had suggested, talking our way into someone's home.

We did some research at the town hall and discussed what to do next. In the syllabus by Prof. John Rassias, there was a chapter called "The Village Drop." It was about two American students who had run out of money in a foreign town. In the story, the students went to the mayor's house and were invited to a great meal and overnight hospitality—a happy ending.

Being the creative students we were, we decided to find out where the mayor lived. We followed directions and walked about a mile to the outskirts of town where we found the mayor's modest farmhouse. We learned he was also the town veterinarian and was not home, but we could wait for him if we wanted to.

When the mayor finally arrived late in the afternoon, we found out disappointingly he had not read Dr. Rassias' book and did not want anything to do with us. Apparently, he did not embrace the biblical call to hospitality. He was a hardworking man in a small town, and he seemed a bit put out by college students who could afford to travel to Europe and were now expecting others to take care of them. No, we could not stay there, and he did not know any place else in town to go if the hotel was full.

Exasperated, he looked up at the steeple a few blocks away and said, "Why don't you try the church?"

Then, he slammed the door. Bob and I looked at each other and without any other options, decided to follow his suggestion. We walked toward the little cathedral. Some dark clouds were starting to form, and we hoped at the very least we could prevail upon the rector to let us sleep at the church if the rain came. A gentle, elderly priest was just finishing a service in the sanctuary. As the few participants left, we approached him and told him our dilemma. We needed a place to stay for the night. The inn was full, and the veterinarian/mayor had not offered us his home or his stable. We were not Joseph or Mary, but he looked at us kindly and led us back to his office.

He apologized but said there was no way we could stay at the church. He started calling several parishioners who evidently all said, "No." We could tell he was getting discouraged that no one would take us in. There was a knock at his door, and he excused himself. Bob and I stayed in his office sharing stories and strategizing our next move. When the priest returned, he had a huge smile on his face. He had found us a place to stay! He went on to say the knock had come from a couple who was getting married the next day. He was going to oversee the rehearsal which was just starting. We were to stay in his office until they were finished. Then, he would walk us down to the restaurant where they were holding the rehearsal dinner. After dinner, the bride would take us back to her home where we could stay for the night. The bride? The night before the wedding? It sounded like a crazy plan to us, but we stayed in his office as he had asked.

An hour later, the priest returned and literally took us by the hand walking us down the main street of Henrichemont, Bob on one side, and me on the other. We headed into an alleyway where he knocked on the screen door that opened to the kitchen of a restaurant. He introduced us to the owner/chef and asked him if he could find us a place to sit and provide a meal for us while we waited for "our ride" who would be in the banquet room.

Bob and I were graciously shown to a small table inside the main room of the small restaurant. The chef was a large jovial man who served us an incredible four-course meal and a bottle of wine. Bob and I were embarrassed, knowing we did have some money, and asked if we could pay for the meal. The chef refused saying we were friends of the priest and his special guests that night. We were now feeling very loved as strangers in this town.

We noticed several very well-dressed people passing our table and heading to the banquet room in the back. A few of them stopped by to say we must be the Americans they had heard about. They had cousins in NY or other places and asked if we knew where those places were. They appeared to be a well-traveled group. Several addressed us in English, which they spoke much better than we could speak French!

A few hours later, the bride and groom came by and excitedly told us to ride with them back to the house. We obediently got in the car, thanking them for their kindness. After a short drive with pleasant conversation, the car pulled into a large estate outside of town. We entered a chateau and came face-to-face with the mother of the bride who evidently had just been alerted of the plan. She was not happy her daughter had offered to put us up for the night. She eyed the two of us in our jeans and sneakers with the same disdain the mayor had. We could understand. Any woman with a house full of family and friends, and a wedding to put on the next day would have done the same. She probably assumed Bob and I were hitchhiking all over Europe together, something she obviously did not approve of; I wouldn't have either.

At the bride's urging, she relented. Someone brought us pillows and blankets, and we were told to head to the Mill House where the groom and best man were staying, a short walk from the main house. Feeling extremely uncomfortable, I wanted to ask the mother if there was any way I could stay in the main house with the bride and her four sisters. The look on her face told me I needed to be grateful for what I had been offered. Bob assured me he would protect me if needed. Thankfully, there was no need. Finding my corner of the room, facing the wall, I quickly fell asleep.

In the morning, everyone was wearing jeans and comfortable clothes and scurrying around. We found out the reception was going to be at the house and on the grounds. There were tents going up and caterers setting up. What had we walked into? Bob and I were willing and able to help with this and the family was grateful. The grey sky of the previous day had given way to bright sunshine. It was May 21, my twentieth birthday. In France, the twentieth birthday is a big celebration comparable to turning twenty-one in the US. Even the mother had begun to smile although I was keeping my distance.

We worked until the wedding party was dressed and ready to head to the village cathedral. Bob and I were going to send them off and hitchhike back to Bourge when the family urged us to get in the car with the parents.

"You are almost like family. Come to the wedding!" they said.

Brushing off my jeans and trying to look as presentable for a wedding as possible, I crammed into the seat next to the mom and Bob climbed in next to me. On the way, they realized they had forgotten to pick up the boutonnieres. Bob and I offered to get them while the family assembled at the church. The mother gave me a grateful look.

After the wedding, they insisted we come back to the reception. Bob and I were treated like special guests of honor. We toasted the bride and groom. They toasted my birthday. We celebrated with them until dusk and realized we really needed to head back to town. Several guests offered to drive us out to the main road. A distinguished-looking couple was leaving at the same time, and

we accepted their invitation. We found out that the husband was a geologist who knew some of the professors at
our college. Such a small world.

We stepped out of their car to cross the street as they
headed north. We looked at each other in amazement and
Bob put his thumb out. We were still laughing about our
last 24 hours when the first car going in our direction
pulled alongside us and asked if we needed a ride. They
took us right to Bob's doorstep in Bourges.

Was this a random set of miracles? I don't think so.
God had answered my prayers for protection. We were
strangers who had been loved and cared for beyond our
wildest imaginations. God intends for His people to be
hospitable. When they are, miracles take place, and people
are blessed, even hitchhiking college students.

Years later as I thought about this story, I realized
Professor Rassias modeled his "village drop" assignment after the pedagogy of another famous teacher: Jesus
of Nazareth. Jesus sent out His disciples two-by-two
instructing them to go to various villages in Israel. They
were told not to take anything for their journey except a
walking stick, but no food, no traveler's bag, no money,
and no change of clothes. Jesus obviously prayed the
people in the towns would be open to hospitality and take
in the strangers. Their assignment was not about practicing their foreign language skills. They were being tested
on their faith and their ability to share the message of the
Good News in their own words.

The disciples were told to accept the hospitality offered them, to heal the sick, and to tell those who would listen about the Kingdom of God coming near. This is how the Gospel story was to be communicated. Person-to-person, home-to-home, town-to-town. For those people and places who did not welcome or listen to the disciples, Jesus gave an ominous warning. He told His followers to, "Shake its dust from your feet as you leave to show you have abandoned those people to their fate" (Mark 6:11 NLT). In Luke's gospel, we hear Jesus saying the fate of those towns would be worse than that of Sodom on judgment day. Sodom was used as the epitome of a sinful and inhospitable town, and it was burned to the ground. The gruesome story is told in Genesis 18 and 19.

On a happier note, like my unexpected invitation to a wedding, Jesus told many stories about wedding feasts, including miracles of provision and of guests showing up who were not on the original invite list. In Matthew 22, He tells a parable indicating that hitchhikers are indeed welcome at the wedding feast He is throwing. In fact, He specifically talks about going to the main roads and bringing any who will come to the feast.

Totally open to unexpected foreigners showing up to my wedding in 1980, I was secretly hoping God would send one or two. To my mother's relief, and my dismay, none showed up.

The morning of my daughter's wedding in 2011 was a different story. There were no hitchhikers, but I came downstairs to a cacophony of sound. It was one of my happiest moments. In my kitchen, surrounded by laughter and chatter in four different languages, Mary Beth was marrying Fernando Jose Puerto Mejia from Honduras. His whole family was staying with us (speaking Spanish), as were Numira, her mother and sister from Kyrgystan (speaking Kyrgyz), and two brothers from Afghanistan (speaking Farsi). English speakers were in the minority, but that was just fine. God was allowing me to repay some of the hospitality that had been extended to me, and it filled me with joy.

You will learn more about some of these wonderful people and how they found their way to the wedding in the next chapter.

Note: The world has changed a lot since 1977. My college dropped "the village drop" as part of the curriculum soon after I had the opportunity to experience it. I do not recommend hitchhiking or picking up strangers if you are alone or at night unless you feel really led to do so. However, I do recommend praying for those strangers you see who may be in need.

Ask Yourself...

Do I think the gospel message would have spread as effectively if Jesus had not sent out His disciples two-by-two?

_____

_____

Jesus spoke frequently at weddings and other feasts. Check out Luke 14 and Matthew 22.

Have I ever followed His instruction and intentionally invited the marginalized who could not repay me? Explain:

_____

_____

Have I ever had someone shut the door to me? How did it feel?

_____

_____

Can I forgive and move on? If not, what do I need to do?

_____

_____

Did it encourage me toward revenge or to greater hospitality? Explain:

_____

_____

Dig Deeper...

Read 3 John 1.

Who is John commending for his hospitality to strangers?

_____

_____

What does this passage say this labor of love was?

_____

_____

Who did John condemn and why?

_____

_____

How does this passage speak to you?

_____

_____

Real, true religion from God the Father's perspective is
about caring for orphans and widows who suffer needlessly....
(James 1:27 VOICE)[6]

CHAPTER 5

International Orphans in Need of a Home

J
ames, the brother of Jesus, tells us true religion includes caring for widows and orphans in their need. One of the most beautiful acts of hospitality is shown when families take in children (and young adults) who need a home whether they need temporary foster care, have been orphaned, or have been given up for adoption for other reasons. Providing a long-term home is very different from taking in a stranger for a night or two. It is so inspiring when families offer their hearts and homes to foster or adopt children. It is something we should heartily support in our communities and churches if we cannot do so ourselves.

The topic of adopting a child came up while Lee and I were dating. Honestly, I suggested it and was more open to the possibility than he was. Several of my friends have been adopted. Other couples I know who have fostered or adopted children have successfully and beautifully woven them into their families. Lee was more aware of some of the unfortunate instances where adoptions did not go well.

He is a realist and I appreciate the balance he provides to my sometimes-unrealistic optimism. In this case, he had a sobering point. Bringing a temporarily or permanently orphaned child into your home is a huge responsibility and commitment. Unless all parties are on board and willing to make the sacrifices necessary to create a safe and loving place for the new family member to feel at home, it is not recommended.

During this time, I began to pray for orphans as part of my regular prayer routine. We had friends who worked with orphans in Central America, who asked us to support them. Along with occasional small donations, I felt the least I could do was support them in prayer.

In the fall of 1985, we were living in Syracuse, NY. Lee was working at the Syracuse Community Health Center. We were placed there to pay back a Public Health Scholarship he had received to cover his medical school expenses. We had two small children at the time, and I was pregnant with our third.

One day, as I was praying for my kids and the orphans in Central America, I heard a distinct voice which I immediately recognized as God's. The conversation went something like this:

Me: "God, please bless...and bless...and bless the orphans in Central America and bless..."

God: "Annie, please stop a minute."

Me: "But God, I'm praying."

God: "Yes, I hear that you are talking, but you are not listening."

(I had not yet learned the importance of prayer being a two-way conversation)

Me: "Oh, I'm sorry. I'm listening now." (I thought prayer was about getting God's attention, not Him getting mine.)

God: "Annie, prayer is good. The children in Central America have many people praying for them. That pleases me. I have a different assignment for you. Are you willing to pray for a different set of orphans?"

Me: (Confused, but willing to listen) "Okay, who and where, Lord?"

God: "There are thousands of orphans in Afghanistan with no one praying for them. Would you begin to spend time praying for them?"

Me: "Afghanistan? I'm a geography major. I will find out. Of course, I will pray for them."

God: "Thank you."

Silence.

Bewildered, I wondered what was going on in Afghanistan. God was obviously concerned about something important. Feeling an urgency to find out, I put the kids in the car and headed to the local library to look up articles on orphans in Afghanistan. (This was pre-Google and home computers.) The Soviets started pulling out of Afghanistan in the early 80s, and they were lacing the fields with land mines. Children walking to school were getting blown up and losing limbs daily. Parents, especially war widows who were unable to support their families, would drop their children at orphanages which were dirty, crowded, and unfit for the hundreds of children packed into them.

My heart broke as I read one article after another about the dire conditions orphaned children were facing. One orphanage was housing over 900 children. There were pictures of more than fifty children packed into a dark room in a facility without adequate sanitation, food, clothing, blankets, or supervision. No wonder God's heart was breaking. Things were desperate in that war-torn nation.

When Lee came home, I announced we needed to adopt an Afghan orphan. He looked at me like I was crazy. He listened patiently while I told him about the message that had interrupted my morning prayers and my trip to the library. He was sympathetic but let me know he had not heard a similar message. Praying for orphans, and adopting them from a foreign country, were two entirely different things. He loved me, loved God, and loved our kids. We had our hands full at the time. He encouraged me to keep praying, and he would let me know if God confirmed anything to him. When I went back to prayer, all I heard was "Keep praying."

God sent a special messenger to Joseph after Mary told him about Gabriel's visit and that she was with child. God wants both parents to be on the same page. Taking on a major responsibility in hospitality like hosting or adopting a baby requires both parties to be in complete agreement. If not, the welcome is not going to be complete.

Years went by. I continued to pray for the orphans and children in Afghanistan. Every now and then, there would be an article in the paper about a child coming to the US for a limb replacement. They had stepped on a land mine on their way to school or while playing in the fields. When I showed the article and picture to Lee, he would note the child was accompanied by at least one parent. No, I should not go to the hospital to meet them. He assured me he was praying, too, but God had not given him release for us to take on an Afghan orphan. I continued to pray for all the orphans in Afghanistan and waited to see if God would have us adopt one in the future.

Nurmira

In 2000, we were living in Orchard Park, NY. Our four children were growing up. We had a reputation for hospitality and being a home where all were welcome. Many young adults had asked to stay with us for a few weeks or months, or however long they needed a place to stay. Usually, they came one at a time and stayed for a set period while they were in transition. One would move out, and another would ask to take their place. Our kids got used to having "bonus" family members around along with the grandparents who were frequent long-term visitors.

One day, I got a call from a friend at church. He asked if we knew anyone willing to take in a young woman from Kyrgyzstan for the summer. We asked for more details. He didn't have many. He said he couldn't really pronounce her name, but she was about twenty years old, played the cello well, spoke very little English, and had no money. She was a religious refugee waiting for the determination of her legal status. She had just finished a semester at a small Bible college, but now had nowhere to go.

Lee agreed we should take Nurmira in since we had the room, and it was only for the summer. As soon as she arrived, we all recognized God had brought her to us as a special gift. The more we learned of her story, the more we were determined to protect her and help her as best we could. Nurmira had arrived in the U.S. a few years earlier. She had become a Christian at the age of thirteen while attending the national music boarding school in Bishkek, the capital of Kyrgyzstan. She was eighteen when she left after being persecuted in her traditionally Muslim home country. As in Afghanistan, once the Soviets pulled out, her nation had returned to its Islamic roots. It was struggling economically and socially as it tried to become an independent republic.

Her journey in the U.S. had started on the West Coast. She had been invited to play her cello for a Russian/Christian youth conference. Her cousin was an underground church youth pastor who had been given scholarships to arrange for several students in Kyrgyzstan to attend the conference. In the end, only Nurmira and her cousin had the documentation that made it possible to travel to the U.S. She had a passport because a few years earlier, as the premier youth cellist in her nation, she had traveled to other countries with the President's wife, showcasing her musical talents to promote Kyrgyz culture. Her government gave her clearance to leave for what she and they assumed was another cultural exchange trip. Her visa came through only days before she was to leave. She packed a few things and said goodbye to her mother, who didn't believe she was really going to the U.S.

Nurmira attended the conference in Seattle and then her cousin told her the full story. He had only bought her a one-way ticket. Nurmira had already been banned from the national orchestra because of her conversion to Christianity. Family and friends had shunned her. There was no way she could excel in her musical gifts if she stayed in Kyrgyzstan. Her cousin arranged for her to stay with some church leaders in the U.S. Then he left, taking the cello she had borrowed from the music school in Bishkek back with him.

Her story about experiencing both hospitality and rejection is its own book. People of many persuasions, mostly Christian, and Jewish, helped her as God directed her path from one home to another across the country, playing her cello and sharing her story. By the time she came to our home, she needed more than a place to stay for a night or a few weeks. She was courageous and filled with faith and hope, but she was weary and uncertain about her future. She had filed for asylum but was still waiting to hear over a year later. She missed her own family but did not feel it was safe to head home. She had made many friends along the way, but still felt like a stranger and nomad. What she really needed now was a deeper level of love and con-nection. She needed to be part of a family and ours was waiting to love her.

A few weeks into her stay with us, Nurmira asked if she could call me mom. At the time, I was reading "The Purpose Driven Life" by Rick Warren. The book challenged me to think about what the phrase "Family of God" really meant. Do we take on family-level responsibilities for those in the "household of God" who need our help? In this case, I was convicted and convinced that I needed to ratchet up my level of hospitality towards Nurmira.

Nurmira needed a family. She also needed a cello. She was a gifted musician without her own instrument to practice on. We loved music and made certain that our own children had suitable instruments to match their level of expertise. One son had an expensive drum set. Another had a great trombone. A third had a decent violin (which he stopped playing in middle school). We had splurged on a nice piano for the house. As I prayed, I felt God tell me to let Nurmira know we were willing to be her American family, and we would help her get a cello.

Nurmira was overjoyed to be welcomed as a family member, but sweetly declined the offer of the cello.

"Thank you, Mom, but you can't afford the type of cello I need."

It quickly became obvious I had never been mom to a concert-level musician. My first thought was she was naive, not understanding U.S. dollars and our economy.

"How much would it cost?" I asked her.

She hesitated, then told me that a student-level, Chinese-made, cello would cost around $6,000, but the kind she needed for concerts cost much more.

"How much more?" I asked.

"Well, my Eastman Music School professor's cello costs about $500,000.00," she said, then quickly added, "I could probably get by with one in the $30,000 range."

She was right about one thing. We couldn't afford to buy her a cello. As I prayed, I sensed an answer from God. Yes, we were to help her get a cello, but not necessarily buy it for her. "How," I asked Him? Hospitality in this case was going to be more costly in some ways than I had expected.

Nurmira had been playing at churches and taking in offerings for her cello for several months. Another musician and some friends arranged for her to record a CD which she would sell when she played. She had saved a few thousand dollars towards the purchase of a cello, but she had a long way to go. As I prayed, I sensed God telling me to arrange a concert in the Buffalo area. She had a gift and a story to be heard by a broader audience. Perhaps, I could get more people to help me love this stranger who had landed on our doorstep.

We called the concert "A Gift of Bows and Strings." Little by little the event came together with a college donating a wonderful concert facility, a printer donating invitations, and good friends donating time and energy to sell tickets and help with set up. The night finally came, and it was wonderful. Nurmira's musical artistry and compelling story brought many to tears.

Donations came in more forms than cash. One Jewish man attended because he really loved cello music and had been invited by a friend he worked out with in a gym. He was an immigration lawyer and was deeply affected by her story. He offered to help Nurmira in any way he could. A beautiful, unexpected blessing! The cash donations totaled around $15,000. Added to her other savings, the 17th-century cello she had eyed at a music store in Rochester was becoming a possibility. The bow would cost an additional $3,000, and the case at least $800. We were still short by about $9,000. Disappointed, I didn't realize God had a surprise for us.

Nurmira had been invited to play a cello solo at a church in the Rochester area the week before the benefit concert. As she played, the pastor was visibly moved. He stood and explained he knew she was trying to purchase her own cello. He invited the congregation to come forward if God was moving them to help her secure an appropriate instrument. Nurmira was stunned as hundreds of parishioners started walking toward her and handing her money. The pastor asked her to play another song. They placed a box at her feet. People kept coming forward. Nurmira had to leave right after the service. The church said they would call her when they had counted the donations and sorted out the checks.

A few days after the Bows and Strings benefit concert, I heard Nurmira screaming with joy into the phone. The Rochester church called to let her know they were writing her a check for almost $9,000. It was the largest "free will" offering they had ever received at the church.

A few weeks later, she purchased a 17th-century Italian cello. She had dreamed of owning one exactly like it, but couldn't imagine it ever really being hers. As her bonus mom, I was happily astonished. God had heard all our prayers and provided through the generosity and obedience of hundreds of people. Every time she plays it, she is reminded of the "family of God" who loved her well, and God's ultimate care for her through His people.

> **God cares about orphans. He knows their needs. It is a privilege to partner with Him in caring for "strangers" He sends our way. Practicing hospitality matters more than you can fathom to those in need.**

More than twenty years later, Nurmira still calls me Mom Annie. Over the span of many years, her own mother and all her siblings have been able to immigrate to the US. She married an American man she met at music school, and they held their reception in our backyard. He put his musical gifts on hold and pursued a law degree and is now an immigration lawyer himself. She performs and teaches music in NYC. They have three awesome children who call us Nonnie Annie and Grandpa Lee. It was a privilege for me to be the birth coach for two of them. (I was out of the country when the third came a week early.)

What started as an offer of hospitality for a few weeks one summer has resulted in a lifelong family relationship.

It wasn't a formal adoption, but it broadened my scope of love for strangers and the family of God and has been a great joy for all of us.

It was also great preparation for what would come next. Kyrgyzstan borders a country that was still on my heart: Afghanistan. The need to pray for orphans there intensified over the next few years.

Then 9/11 Happened

Nurmira had been part of the family for over a year when 9/11 occurred. I was distraught when I learned many of the dissident foot soldiers in Osama Bin Laden's army in Afghanistan had been recruited from the crowded Afghan orphanages. It made me feel I had not prayed nearly enough for the orphans and children of that nation during the previous sixteen years.

Three years later, in 2004, I received a call from a teacher who taught at the high school my youngest boys were attending. He was looking for a family who would be willing to host a fifteen-year-old male Afghan student who would be a junior at the high school through a State Department Program called the YES program. The program relied on former Peace Corps volunteers, like himself, to help place thirty promising Afghan high school juniors (fifteen girls and fifteen boys) across the U.S. for twelve months. All the students were carefully vetted from families who had refugeed in Pakistan during the Taliban rule and had now returned to Afghanistan to rebuild their nation. Host families quickly volunteered to help the girls. It had been widely publicized how Afghan women were not receiving fair educations under the previous Taliban rule.

Fifteen-year-old Afghan males were harder to place. The U.S. and local news had been filled with stories of fifteen-year-old boys joining the terrorist groups. The Peace Corps and our teacher had run out of families to call. All had said "No." They were not willing to take the risk. He had heard we had recently housed someone from Kyrgyzstan. The countries were neighbors. Surely, we wouldn't be afraid to host an Afghan student.

Explaining the situation to my husband, to my surprise he answered, "Maybe this is the Afghan orphan you have been praying about."

Telling the teacher I would call him back, I went to my room and prayed to God. This had to be verified by God himself, and not just an emotional response from me.

> Me: "I think this kid has parents; does he count as an orphan? I wasn't planning on a government program, is this really from You?"

> God: "Yes, did I put parameters on my assignment for you?"

Me: "No, you did not. I think I may have put my own twist on things."

God: "You do that sometimes."

Me: Cringe.

God: "This young man needs a host family for a year. Your husband is on board. Are you willing to accept him as a son for as long as I ask?"

Me: "Yes Lord."

The answer came with a sense of confirmation and peace. This young man did not fit my definition of an orphan, but God was using the U.S. State Department to place him in our home. He needed a host family. We were to take him in and offer him hospitality.

Hanan arrived in August. He seemed a perfect fit for us lining up between our son Chris who was a senior and Mark who was a freshman. He had a great sense of humor and was used to a busy household with lots of family and friends coming and going. We had an incredible year together. We respected his conservative Muslim faith, and he respected our conservative Christian faith. We learned a lot from each other. There are no words to describe how special that year was.

We cried when we had to send him off the following July. His suitcase was full of presents for his family, especially for his mother, whom Hanan spoke of constantly. He was returning home to live in his parents' house along with the family of many of his siblings and their children. He was the youngest by seven years compared to his other five siblings, and the only one unmarried.

He couldn't wait to get back and see his mom. She was a school principal, and she was the one who wanted him to have this adventure in America. They were very close. A brother in Afghanistan had called a few weeks earlier to tell him their mother would not be at home the day he arrived back in Kabul. She had been chosen for a special pilgrimage to Mecca in which participants were not allowed to communicate with the outside world for several weeks. Hanan was disappointed but could easily believe it. He had told me about what a devout and generous woman she was. The gifts he had bought for her could wait until she got back from her pilgrimage.

We hoped we would see Hanan again, but the program participants had to agree to spend at least two years back in Afghanistan before they would be allowed to return to the US for any reason. The point of the program was to teach these talented young people about democracy, to "undemonize" the impression many Afghans had of Americans and vice versa, and to let them be ambassadors to and for their nation.

About a week after sending Hanan back to Kabul, I received a phone call from a man who identified himself as Hanan's uncle. He sadly related that Hanan's mother was not actually on a pilgrimage. She had died several weeks earlier of a medical procedure gone wrong. She was 47, my age at the time. They had withheld the information from Hanan at the time, knowing his grief would be intense and there was no family to comfort him. He would be devastated. With only a few weeks left of the program, they decided to wait until his scheduled return to share the news when they could be with him. That day had come. Now, they were calling us to thank our family for taking such good care of Hanan during his year in the US.

He reported that Kabul was still in a state of disrepair. The electricity and infrastructure were spotty. The schools were terrible. Teachers only showed up occasionally. There was inconsistent instruction and a lack of structure altogether. He also reported he knew Hanan was despondent without his mother. His year away had changed him in many ways and he was feeling very much alone.

I was tearing up, knowing Hanan's tender heart, when the uncle asked me a stunning question. "Would you consider adopting Hanan?"

Standing with the phone in my hand, I wondered if I heard him correctly. He was waiting for an answer. When I blurted out yes, I had no idea if it was even possible. He thanked me and said we would be in touch.

Lee was in Honduras at the time on a medical mission, and I was unable to talk to him until later in the evening. We prayed and pondered the long-term consequences of saying yes, but still felt the peace to do so. We knew one of the main reasons the family wanted us to take him was the assumption that we would have the resources to help Hanan finish both a high school and college education. They loved him and wanted a better life for him. We did, too.

His father was still alive, but infirmed and elderly. With Hanan's family's blessing, we explored what would happen next. An official adoption was not possible due to two factors. Hanan had just turned sixteen and was too old for an international adoption according to U.S. law at the time. Also, Afghanistan was a Muslim nation and did not allow Christian families to adopt Muslim children.

More than twenty years after God had first put Afghan children on my heart and prayer list, we were given a chance to show our love for one young man in a personal way, for a lifetime. Not as part of a government program for a year, but as a member of our family for as long as God saw fit. Only He could have arranged these circumstances.

We realized this was to be a heart adoption. It was not an *illegal* one, just not a usual one in the eyes of many. Hanan was not allowed to return to the U.S. for two years, but the family was willing to let us step in right away. With their permission, we enrolled him in a private international school in Kabul where he could finish his senior year and work on SAT prep. After graduating from high school there, he got a scholarship to a college in the U.S. and returned on a student visa. He earned a degree in engineering, and after working for several years, became a legal U.S. citizen.

Afghans have close family ties and so do we. Our "heart adoption" extended to his brother Ab who was living alone in Toronto, Canada. He was seven years older and had arrived prior to 9/11 with the help of a UN program. We had met him the first year Hanan was with us on the YES program. Ab was in the process of becoming a Canadian citizen but could not yet cross the US border. We could. We helped the brothers wave to each other across the Niagara River in Niagara Falls, give gifts (that we transported across the border), and exchange virtual hugs. Ab called me on Mother's Day the first year Hanan was with us. He posed a question: since I was Hanan's host mother for the year and he was Hanan's brother, would I allow him to call me mom, too?

Later, I learned Ab was aware his mother had died when he called me that first Mother's Day. He was grieving alone in Toronto and in need of family love. He had been on his own journey for several years, leaving the family in Pakistan where they were refugees during the height of the first Taliban invasion in the early '90s. He had joined a UN program hoping to find a nation that would be a safe refuge for his whole family. The UN placed him in Indonesia before sending him to Canada. This was all prior to 9/11 and the family being able to go back to Afghanistan. He wanted to fulfill his mother's dream of a safe haven for the family, and now she was gone.

God gave us a special love and place in our family for both brothers. Their primary allegiance is to their birth family, as it should be, while continuing special relationship with us. To this day, both Ab and Hanan call me on Mother's Day, and keep in touch on a regular basis. Years later, I was able to be with Ab and his wife the day they welcomed their first son into their family. They now have three children. More bonus grandkids!

In the last four years, the remaining four siblings of these brothers and their families have all found refuge in safe countries. One family is in Germany, one is in France, three are in Canada, and Hanan is in the U.S.

Watching this family survive inhospitable places has taught me so much:

- ❖ I have seen the pain when families get torn apart.
- ❖ I have seen what war does to a nation.
- ❖ I have seen the hardship many go through just to survive.
- ❖ I have seen the sadness of children who have lost one or both parents.
- ❖ My awareness of suffering has increased.
- ❖ My heart for orphans in any and every country has grown.

❖ I have become more aware of how many children and young people in our own nation need adoption or foster care.

❖ I have seen what a warm smile and welcome can do to comfort them.

These people in need that I was becoming more aware of are all children of God. He has a good plan for each of their lives and we can be a part of helping them thrive. Foster families that I know have told me how seldom they get invited to someone's home for fear the kids they have taken in might be a bad influence, because of the hard life they have already lived. *Can we take more risks here?*

Families who have adopted children can also use our help. Rather than just admiring them, we can extend love to make sure each child knows they are loved in their new community.

Ask Yourself...

What are my thoughts on adoption (formal or informal) and foster care?

_____

_____

Has my family ever considered adoption or foster care? Explain:

_____

_____

What does "Family of God" mean to me?

_____

_____

Where do hospitality and adoption intersect?

_____

_____

Do I know a family who has adopted or fostered children?

_____

_____

How can I make an effort to get to know these families and see if there are ways to help and support them and the children they are caring for?

_____

_____

Dig Deeper...

Read James 1:27 in various Bible translations.

Write and memorize the translation that gives you the most insight.

_____

_____

Write out what this verse means to you and explain why it is so important to understand God's heart for orphans.

_____

_____

_____

_____

"I was a stranger and you welcomed me."
– Matthew 25:35 (ESV)

Chapter 6

Sojourners and Other Strangers

Have you ever been a stranger traveling alone in a foreign country?

A s I mentioned in a previous chapter, in the spring of 1977 I was in France for a study abroad program. While there, I experienced my own desperate need for love and protection as a stranger. I did not know that along with some French language and culture, I would be learning lifelong lessons by encountering circumstances that made me dependent on the hospitality of others.

Before classes started, a friend and I traveled together using our Eurail passes to hop on and off in many cities throughout Europe. After our travels, I headed off to study in Bourge in central France. She was in a different program in Toulouse in the south of France. We decided I would come south to visit her when I had a free weekend. A few weeks into the term, I sent her an airmail letter letting her know I was coming. Although I didn't hear back, I assumed she had gotten my letter, so I made my train reservations and packed an overnight bag expecting to arrive on a Saturday afternoon. Assuming I would be eating with her host family and could cash a check if I needed it, I brought travelers' checks but very little cash.

What I didn't know was there had been a postal strike which it turns out was quite common in France. Therefore, she never got my letter, and she was not there to greet me at the station. After nervously waiting 20 minutes, I pulled out a list of phone numbers of the host families where the students in the program were staying. Using the pay phone at the train station, I called her number first. No answer there or with the next several numbers I called. Finally, I connected with one family who informed me this was a holiday weekend, and most of the students, including the one staying with them, were probably traveling with their host families.

Alone in a strange city with no plan and no money, I prayed God would guide and protect me and show me what to do next. Desperately, I dialed my friend's number one more time with my last franc. Still no answer, but as I hung up, a strange thing happened. Instead of my one-franc piece coming out, a five-franc piece dropped into my hand. Now I had $1.25 to spend. A warm sense came over me that God was going to be my host in Toulouse and oversee the provision for my needs.

Leaving the train station, I checked to see if any banks were open so I could cash a check, but they were all closed for the holiday weekend. The next train back to Bourge did not leave until the following afternoon. Walking to several hotels near the station, I asked if they would take a traveler's check. The first few said no. Probably sounding a bit desperate, at last, one desk clerk said she might consider it. The woman explained she and her husband owned the small hotel. He was away for a few hours, but she would have to check with him before she could give me a final answer. She suggested I come back later. Thanking her, I headed to a large park in front of the train station.

As I sat thinking and praying about what to do next, I noticed a very "creepy guy" looking in my direction and closing in on me. It was obvious I was a tourist and alone, at least for the time being. Glancing around, I saw an elderly peasant woman, sitting on a bench across the park. She was short and hunched over, dressed in dark clothing with a scarf wrapped around her head like many of the older woman I had seen. Quickly standing up and heading toward her, I was hoping soon to be in the safety of the older woman. As I approached her, she rose from her bench, and I felt my heart sink for a moment thinking she was about to leave. I would have to find a different safe place. Instead of leaving, she looked up at me, grinned broadly with her finely lined face, and motioned me to sit down next to her.

She patted my arm and began talking rapidly in French saying she lived nearby. She asked about who I was, why I was there, and I related my story of being alone in the city. After a while, she looked down at the little bag she was carrying. She said I must be hungry. Although I was hungry, I didn't want to admit it. She smiled again and unfolded another plastic bag. She took out a baguette of bread, carefully broke it in half, and insisted I take one of the pieces. Not sure what to do or say, I numbly held the bread in my hand before she placed it in what was now to be my lunch bag. With a satisfactory smile on her face, she pulled out a small package holding four slices of cheese. She rewrapped two of them and gave them to me for my bag. Next, she pulled out two bananas and broke them apart...giving me one.

By now, I was starting to cry, embarrassed to take anything from this poor woman who I assumed was a widow. However, she kept grinning and patting my arm in a reassuring way. It was giving her great joy to help the frightened American college student. We laughed and chatted for a while longer until she sighed and said she had to go. Collecting my thoughts and trying to figure out if I should give the food back, she got up, hugged me, and hurried around a corner.

Humbled by this woman's offering to me, I noticed the "creepy guy" had wandered off and out of the park as soon as the older woman had begun to engage with me. God was surely looking out for me. This might sound strange, but it occurred to me this woman might have been an angel. To this day, I still think that might be the case. Something supernatural was happening. First, the five-franc-piece, and now this encounter in the park.

My confidence in God's provision was growing, and He was using the hospitality of others to care for me.

Deciding to head towards the hotel where the husband had now returned, they affirmed they would be able to take a traveler's check for a night's lodging. The wife remembered I didn't have any cash and thoughtfully asked if I was hungry and needed food. She invited me for dinner, but I told them I was fine and just wanted to rest. Instead, they asked me to join their family for breakfast the next morning, and I gladly accepted that offer. I went to my small room, ate my cheese and bread and banana, and thanked God for providing for me in mysterious and perfect ways.

The next morning, I was invited into a lovely room where the proprietors and their children were eating breakfast. It was Sunday and I wanted to find a church where I could thank God for taking such good care of me, so I asked if they knew where any evangelical churches met. They had no idea, but they handed me the newspaper and told me to look for a church there. They were Catholic as most of the people in Toulouse were and proudly pointed to the Cathedral which could be seen through their front windows. Not knowing how to find or get to any other places of worship, I finished breakfast, thanked them for their kindness, and headed toward the cathedral. The other cathedrals and churches I had visited in the past months were cold, dark, and empty except for a few older men and women who all seemed to dress in drab colors. This one was different.

The Cathedral of Saint Stephen is an immense cathedral with origins in the 11th and 12th centuries. The magnificent stained glass is some of the oldest in Toulouse and the church has a fascinating history having withstood fires, wars, and several rebuilds. More than the exquisite architecture, I was immediately impressed by the crowd of young and old, including whole families, singing hymns and creating an atmosphere of joy inside the sanctuary. It was warm and welcoming. The cathedral seemed filled with the Holy Spirit and the presence of God.

When the service was over, I was so moved I felt I had to express my thanks to someone, but who? There was a long procession of priests and deacons led by the archbishop, filing down the center aisle and around the back of the church. Before I quite knew what I was doing, I caught the robe of the last one in line, a young-looking deacon. Enthusiastically, I expressed my gratefulness for the chance to experience the worship that morning. He looked at me and without hesitation, asked if he could introduce me to the archbishop and relate the things I had just told him. Before I knew what to say, I was meeting in the back of the cathedral with the archbishop, a gentle older man, small in physical stature, but large with his mitered hat and authority. He thanked me for my comments and asked why I was in Toulouse. I blurted out an abridged version of the postal strike, my failed meet-up with a friend, and my surprise at finding the banks closed so I was unable to cash a check.

He looked at me thoughtfully, and responded, "Then you probably have no money and no place for lunch. I would love for you to join us at the rectory after the noon Mass." Stunned, I awkwardly accepted the invitation with no idea of what to expect.

As I walked the city streets for the next hour, I felt songs in French bubbling up in my heart praising God. Laughing to myself, I realized it was Pentecost after all, the same day the Holy Spirit had descended on the disciples in the upper room and gave them the ability to speak in tongues of different languages to the pilgrims visiting Jerusalem. Stopping at a payphone, I called my friend's number one more time. No answer, so I dialed the next number and surprisingly got an answer. Jessie had just returned to Toulouse from the holiday weekend. Although I did not know her well, she immediately invited me to meet her for lunch. When I told her about my interesting lunch plans with the archbishop, we agreed to meet later in the afternoon.

Back at the cathedral, I knocked on the rectory door and I was let in by an older woman who looked at me a bit suspiciously. Then she led me to an elegant dining room where I was given a seat around a large table with twelve priests. All I can say about the meal is that the bishops eat well in France. It was a delicious meal. Oddly, even though the priests acknowledged me kindly with nods of their heads, no one spoke to me. It was a bit awkward being the only woman at the table, but considering the circumstances, I was honored to be at the table and offered such a lovely feast. When the meal was over, the housekeeper showed me to the door, and that was that. It was strange to receive such lovely and amazing hospitality in a place I never expected to find it.

Full of the story of God's provision for me, a lonely stranger in a strange city, I set off to meet with Jessie. As we walked and talked all afternoon, it became clear to me God loved Jessie very much. She was going through a time of serious discouragement. He knew she needed a friend to encourage her in life and faith as much as I did. Afterward, it dawned on me that God had known all about the postal strike and that my friend would not get my letter. He let me go anyway because He was concerned about Jessie and had lessons to teach me I could not have learned otherwise. This particular weekend was as much about His love for Jessie as it was about His love for me. God's provision for me came through the practice of biblical hospitality surprisingly showered on me by a poor widow, an innkeeper and his wife, an archbishop, and another student who needed encouragement.

It was humbling to be reminded that my story is always a small part of a bigger story. Yours is, too! In the years since that experience, I get an excited feeling when I find myself in strange places lacking my own resources. Having experienced the radical hospitality of others, I know God will somehow provide. The kind of "know that I know that I know" deep in my heart. Daily I pray I can be a blessing to those who extend hospitality to me, and that I am ready to extend it to sojourners who cross my path at unexpected times and places.

Being invited to the table with the archbishop and priests on Pentecost Sunday reminds me of how twelve-year-old Jesus was welcomed to sit and converse with leaders of the temple while his parents frantically searched for him. Although no one was looking for me, the religious leaders had invited me to sit down with them and I knew I was just where my heavenly Father had planned for me to be on that day.

Paul the Apostle was delayed and waylaid on several of his journeys. He always ended up exactly where God wanted him, whether through a shipwreck, or other means, even in prison. Through the hospitality of the people he met, Paul survived, and God's kingdom was strengthened. My prayer is that as His people, we can continue practicing hospitality and strengthening the kingdom in similar ways.

Ask Yourself…

Was I ever traveling and found myself in a situation where I lacked resources and had to depend on strangers to meet my needs?

_____

_____

Did I ask God for help? If so, how did He answer my prayer?

_____

_____

Am I willing to rejoice and trust God when He interrupts my travel plans?

_____

_____

Have I ever received material provisions or gifts from someone of less means than me? If so, how did it make me feel?

_____

_____

Have I been willing to show hospitality when the giving comes out of my lack of sufficiency and not just from my abundance?

_____

_____

Dig Deeper...

Several biblical stories of God's supernatural provision come to mind as I think of my visit to Toulouse. One example is when the disciples panicked because they saw the number of people listening to Jesus and realized He was asking the twelve of them to feed the crowd (Matthew 14:13-21). Biblical hospitality resulted in miraculous provision.

My interaction with the older woman in the park reminds me of the widow who generously gave her two copper coins at the temple. God was more pleased with her offering than that of those who gave out of their plenty. The bread, cheese, and banana I received from the woman on the bench are some of the most extravagant gifts of hospitality I have ever received. I want to be willing to give that generously, especially to strangers.

Read: Matthew 15:32-39 and Mark 12:41-44

Jesus multiplied five loaves of bread and two fish in Matthew 15 to make them enough to satisfy thousands of people.

Who shared from his lack to serve Jesus?

_____

_____

What was the response from the crowd?

_____

_____

The widow gave her mite at the temple in generous giving to supply the needs of the temple community in Mark 12.

What did Jesus say about this to His disciples?

_____

_____

How do these passages speak to you?

_____

_____

_____

_____

Hospitality often demands risk-taking and sacrifice.
It takes generosity, kindness, and perseverance.
But what a difference it makes in the world!

CHAPTER 7

Refugees and Immigrants in Our Country and Communities

The stranger who dwells among you shall be to you as one born among you, and you shall love him as yourself; for you were strangers in the land of Egypt: I am the LORD your God. (Leviticus 19:33-34 NKJV)

In October of 2019, Ab and his wife Bekah excitedly called from Toronto to tell us that Bekah's father, mother, and three younger siblings, aged nineteen, fourteen, and ten, were coming to America! They received special immigrant visas because her father worked with the U.S. forces following the 9/11 bombings, and this put the family at risk while remaining in Afghanistan. They would arrive by the end of the month, following what had been a several-year application process. Sadly, Bekah's two older brothers were older than twenty-one when the process was started, so they were not allowed to come with the rest of the family. As the Taliban forces grew in numbers, they would be left behind in a nation growing increasingly hostile to democracy and those who aided the United States.

The family asked to be placed in a U.S. city near Toronto with a relocation office that processed immigrants and refugees. They wanted to be near their eldest daughter Bekah and their two grandchildren. Only an international bridge crossing and a three-hour drive would separate them! The father longed for his two younger daughters to be well-educated. He dreamed for his youngest son to learn and play freely and not be forced to live under Taliban rules. He had lived through that horror once before. His family had sought refugee status in Pakistan for many years prior to 9/11 because of a previous Taliban takeover.

The terms immigrant, refugee, and asylum seeker, are technically and legally different even though most of us confuse them. They all involve people leaving their home country and moving to another for any number of reasons. In our country, Immigrants are people who have been well-vetted by America while still residing in their home country or a safe second country. They usually apply under specific programs created by the American government, often in gratitude for the applicant's service to the U.S.A. This service for the US Government often puts them in danger, especially as the US draws down operations in the foreign country.

Refugees often apply through UN humanitarian programs in third countries, or just look for admission once they reach a border crossing. Asylum seekers are often those who may have entered legally on a visitor, work, or student visa, but now wish to stay due to various changes or dangers in their home country. Refugees who cross a border illegally must also go through the asylum process. Many are turned back. Immigrants arrive with social security cards, green cards (work visas), and temporary help with healthcare, food, and housing, and employment. They are put on a 5–7-year track to citizenship. They are allowed to apply to bring other close relatives (older sons and daughters, elderly parents, spouses, grandchildren, and siblings), but those applications go into files and the wait can be up to twelve or more years. It is an anxious process. Families are often torn apart and scattered for decades. Bekah's family members were coming as legal immigrants.

We were able to greet Bekah's family when they arrived in the US. Ab and Bekah came down from Toronto with their kids and it was a joyous reunion. The family was temporarily housed in a lovely Residence Hotel suite for a week until a local resettlement agency had an apartment ready for them. So far, life in America looked beautiful and safe. There were four resettlement agencies in the region at the time, and all were working hard to help immigrants and refugee families adjust to America on a person-by-person basis.

The layers of government oversight and hands-on work are complicated and confusing. The process includes translators, social workers, case workers, educators, housing specialists, and more. When a family is given the green light to arrive in the U.S., the local agencies are often given only short notice to find an appropriate apartment, furnishings, and staff to service their needs.

Unfortunately, for Bekah's family, housing was in short supply when they arrived. They were placed in a low rent apartment on the second floor of a run-down house in a rough area of the city to be near bus lines and the refugee processing center. The stairs up to the second floor were crooked and rickety. They had neither heat nor hot water for the first few days after being dropped off by the resettlement agency. The landlord said he would fix the problem "soon". The agency left some space heaters and hot water pots. It was cold that October and the family would bundle up in several layers to keep warm. It was a devastating reality check after the nice hotel suite.

There was an immigrant family from Africa living in the apartment below and the smells were quite different than anything they were used to. To us, all immigrants have something in common, so we assume they are comfortable being housed together. That is not always the case. There are huge language and cultural differences. Bekah's mother did not speak English. She was frightened and distraught. She had left her nice comfortable home and her two oldest sons and aging parents for this! She cried often and was miserable.

Ab and Bekah called us and begged us to help her family. Could we find them a different place to live and visit them on a regular basis? There was a need beyond the assigned agency workers to come alongside the new family. These strangers were disoriented, alone, and scared. They needed to be loved. The agency was doing all they could, but they were limited. They had several other families who were arriving, too, each with specific and pressing needs.

My practice of hospitality was being stretched in a new way when I entered the world of immigrant and refugee resettlement. I saw firsthand the fear, confusion, and pain along with the gratefulness and joy these families experience in their first weeks, months, and years in America. It is rarely easy for them. Even if one family member is adjusting well, there is usually at least one who is struggling. Some have come from years in refugee camps and are grateful for the little they are offered. Others have come from beautiful homes. Almost all have left most of their belongings behind and traveled with only a few changes of clothes, perhaps a favorite cooking vessel, and a few pictures of home.

As I looked for a new place for them to live, I also learned firsthand the challenge of finding good affordable housing in safe areas. For this first year, they needed to be able to walk or take a city bus to stores, classes, work, and healthcare. So many challenges! The father had brought some cash, but the banks would not allow him to obtain any type of credit card for the first year. The rental agencies would not let him sign a lease without a co-signer. The agencies sign the leases for the apartments they find. If you want to move, they give you a stipend, and you are on your own. We finally found them a side-by-side duplex someone had just flipped. It was clean, although the floors sloped a bit, and the walls were thin. Bekah's mom was happy and grateful. She felt she could breathe for the first time in many weeks.

Then a new curve ball hit us all. Covid 19 became a full-blown global pandemic. The bridge to Canada was closed to non-emergency traffic for almost two years. The schools where the two youngest kids were finally starting to feel a degree of comfort shut down and went to online learning. Job opportunities for the dad were looking bleak as they were for many Americans. We helped him get a driver's license. He had one in Afghanistan, but road rules, stop lights and signs don't mean much there. If a traffic offense occurs, bribing officers is the norm, but I told him that would not be a good thing to try here.

As he drove my car to the test spot on a frigid winter morning, I went over the rules of the road and hoped for the best. Left standing on the side of the road in the freezing cold while Bekah's dad took off in my car with the licensing officer, I remember wondering what I was doing there. Oh right...practicing hospitality! Thankfully, they came back sooner than expected. Abdul had passed. Later that week, Lee helped him negotiate buying a used car. The salesman had never had anyone want to pay cash and it took us a while to convince him it was legitimate.

The dad went to work driving DoorDash and Uber. The oldest daughter got a job at a coffee shop she could walk to. She took ESL classes and helped with the household chores. She took the early morning shift leaving the house in the dark around 5 a.m. and walking the cold snowy streets of the city so she could help the family the rest of the day.

Bekah's mom was able to buy a used sewing machine and she began sewing for the family. This was early on during the COVID-19 pandemic when personal protection gear (PPE) was hard to come by. When I told her the health care center near their house needed masks and headwear, she eagerly volunteered to help. She made thousands of masks with donated material, staying up late at night to get the next batch done.

With the world shut down, the family did not have a chance to meet many new people. We became their Covid-19 pod and they became ours. As the months passed, these strangers became our good friends. They did find others who extended hospitality in life-changing ways. The workers at a local Christian Community Health Center helped in any way they could. A non-profit women's group helped refugees and immigrants by offering sewing classes, used machines, and job opportunities. They soon had Bekah's mom taking sewing jobs where she could make money and spend a few days a week helping other refugee women at the center.

With the help of many hospitable people, these strangers to America assimilated beautifully despite the pandemic. By the end of the first year, they were offering gracious hospitality to us with beautifully arrayed snacks and lavish meals. We celebrated birthdays and holidays together. We shared our traditions with them, and they shared theirs with us. We had lots of fun sledding in the winter, picnicking at Niagara Falls in the spring, and swimming in the summer at a neighbor's pool. None of the kids had ever been in a pool. Fazli, the youngest son took to it like a fish. Two years later, he was winning races on the swim team at school!

By the spring of 2021, the pandemic was waning. The world was opening a bit. President Biden announced U.S. troops were going to pull out of Afghanistan completely by September 11, 2021. Bekah's mom begged her husband to let her take the oldest daughter, now twenty and engaged to a man in Kabul, and the other two siblings back to Afghanistan to see the older brothers and her parents because this might be the last opportunity for many years.

The dad had been unable to secure a credit card for more than $500, so he came over one night in June and asked if I would help him buy the tickets online. He had the cash to pay me back. It was expensive to buy four round-trip tickets, but he felt it was the right thing to do. We booked the tickets, departing in July and returning on August 26, giving them as much time as possible to be with family and friends before school started back in the States. Bekah's dad planned to work day and night to make more money while the family was visiting Afghanistan for the summer.

On August 14, I got a call from a college friend who worked for the State Department and happened to be married to a high-ranking US official in Afghanistan. She had tried to help us get the older brothers out as we saw the political situation deteriorating. She was calling to tell me that Biden had moved up the exit date and it looked like Kabul was going to fall within 24 hours. When I told her about Bekah's mom and siblings who were still visiting in Kabul, she suggested I get them out as soon as possible. The embassy staff had evacuated weeks earlier.

After staying up all night trying to change the reservations, the earliest flight I could get for them (for a huge change fee) was four days later, but as it turned out, that was too late. By the next morning, Kabul had been taken over by the Taliban forces. Thousands were flocking to the airport. U.S. forces had secured the airport, but the Taliban had it surrounded. Commercial flights ceased immediately, and President Biden decided to speed up the withdrawal.

For the next two weeks chaos ensued. Those with U.S. Citizenship were given priority, which was appropriate, and directed to board secured armored buses to be safely transported into the airport compound. 120,000 people were evacuated in this manner. However, Bekah's family were LPRs (Lawful Permanent residents) and not full citizens, so they were left on their own to try to get into the airport. Working day and night with the two older brothers who were forced to trust me, I passed on any information I thought would be helpful and not put them in more danger. We were given airport gate numbers for the family to reach and supposedly be allowed airport entry. Unfortunately, on their first two attempts, they arrived to find the gates either locked, unattended, or incorrect. Meanwhile, buses would show up in their neighborhood to transport approved travelers, but not allow the LPRs to board.

On their third attempt to get the family into the airport in Kabul, they got as far as a few feet from an entrance when the youngest son got hit by shrapnel. The crowds were packed, panicky, unruly, and unsafe. The son's head was bleeding. The younger sister lost her shoe as the brothers tried to rush them away from the gate, off the streets, and back to the protection of their apartment. Then on August 26th, a day the family decided to not go to the gates because of the tremendous and unruly crowds, rioting broke out at the airport. Thirteen U.S. soldiers were killed along with 170 Afghans. Some of the dead were friends and relatives of the family. On August 30, 2021, the last official U.S. plane left Afghanistan. Bekah's family had been left behind.

Alone in the U.S.A., Bekak's dad was numb and hardly able to think. He felt helpless and hopeless. He feared he had sent his whole family to their doom. He had no contacts in Afghanistan that he could trust. With desperation in his eyes, he asked if we would continue to work to find a way for his family to return to America. By God's grace, I stayed in contact with his family in Kabul night after night (there was a twelve-hour time difference). Electricity and cell service could be cut off by the Taliban at any time. The brothers were wisely moving the family from place to place because the Taliban were going door to door looking for Americans and American sympathizers.

Loving strangers takes on a desperate importance when others are hating them and literally looking to kill them. Living the nightmare with them but from the extreme luxury and safety of my own home, I could not give up on them. Given a code name in Farsi, I could securely communicate with the oldest brother and not be questioned if his phone was taken.

We networked with many others trying to help those stranded. Some people were helping out of love, some out of duty, and some out of mercenary motives. Many people were facing dire situations as they tried to flee the country. Young women were being taken from buses and cars headed for border areas and raped. Others were being killed. It was heartbreaking and exhausting.

Then the miracle we and so many others had been praying for happened. We connected with a group of former U.S. military veterans. They had contacts and relationships with local leaders in the northern city of Mazar-i-Sharif. If the family could get to that city, there was a chance they could be flown to safety. It was a risky seven-hour drive over bad roads. However, the alternative of remaining in hiding in Kabul seemed riskier.

The older brothers rented a car and prepped the family on where to hide their documents. If they got stopped, they would tell the authorities they were visiting relatives in the area. They headed north to Mazar-i-Sharif for a safe house the non-profit organization had rented. By the time our family reached the city, the first safe house had been breached. They were told to lay low until a new safe house could be secured. They checked into a hotel, locking the mom and siblings in a room while the brothers ventured out to find food. They moved to a new safe house, and then another.

Three days later, after two attempts to get through the gates at the northern airport, I got a call from my contacts at the non-profit. The plane was in the air! The family was on their way to safety, but there was more good news. The miracle we had prayed for but not believed could happen had come to pass. With only preliminary documents in hand, the two older brothers were on board the plane and on their way to safety, too. The day was September 24, 2021. The family was flown to Abu Dhabi where they were to be housed at the Emirates Humanitarian City for a "few weeks."

On October 14, 2021, after much negotiating, the mom and the three young adults with LPR status were allowed to return to America. The older sons were held at the facility and were not allowed to leave the grounds until August 2022. They reunited with the U.S. family on August 9, 2022, a week shy of a year after the crisis began.

Sharing these details of one family's story is to illustrate the reality of persecution, war, and poverty. Their terror is real. According to a UN refugee agency, there were 27 million refugees worldwide in 2020. Most of them are in Europe, Asia, and Africa. The U.S. plans to officially welcome 125,000 immigrants to America in 2023 from various countries, and only a small portion will be from Afghanistan. This total number pales in comparison to the migrant encounters at the southern border which were running higher than 200,000 per month in 2023. Clearly, for as many as we see coming to our cities and towns, many more are getting turned away.

There is a refugee crisis in America and across the globe. There is no way we as individuals can fix all of it. The world is broken. Our policies are broken. Our cities are broken and needy without adding more strangers. Individual stories can be complicated. How do we know who is safe to cross our borders and who is really in need of safety and protection? The resettlement process is confusing and difficult. Amid this chaos and confusion, can Christian hospitality play a part?

My hope is that you and I can remember that the real definition of hospitality is loving strangers. How we do that regarding foreigners in our country is just as unique as each one of us and our circumstances.

In a recent article, I read about a man in a refugee camp in an African Muslim country who had been imprisoned for four years because of his Christian faith. When he finally got out, he became a pastor in his refugee community. He attended a course on generosity and was convinced he was not only in a place to receive, but to give. He prayed about what he had to give and recognized he had at least two shirts, one more than he needed. He encouraged his refugee church community to think about being generous as well. They showed up the next Sunday with a mountain of clothes that was then delivered to prisons and camps with a greater need than their own.

Hospitality often demands risk-taking and sacrifice.
It takes generosity, kindness, and perseverance.
But what a difference it makes in the world!

God provides for our family as we extend ourselves to love the strangers He puts in our path.

Today, Bekah's family has been in the U.S. for over four years. All the able adults are working to support their family. Two members are working at the Christian Health Clinic: one as a receptionist and trained doula, the other as a case worker. Bekah's mom has an Etsy store where she sells her clothing and crafts. She also helps teach other refugee women to sew and helps newly arrived families adjust to the U.S. The dad continues to drive for Uber and DoorDash. They are good citizens and good neighbors.

The youngest daughter was named student of the month and made the National Honor Society at her public high school. The youngest son has excelled at school and in sports. The father's dream for his family is being realized day by day and week by week.

My own family has been enriched beyond measure by our friendship with these people who were once strangers. We are no longer strangers. We are friends in the truest sense of the word.

The stories of the good Samaritan and Jesus's encounter with the Samaritan woman at the well illustrate the power of loving a stranger from a different background who most people would consider an enemy. In the New Testament, Samaritans and Jews were neighbors geographically, but not friends. Both biblical stories involve the key subject of crossing into foreign territory.

In the story of the good Samaritan, Jesus highlights the hospitality and humanity of the Samaritan over the Jewish men, who walked around the man in need. In the story of the woman at the well, Jesus crosses into foreign territory and engages with a Samaritan woman, much to the surprise and discomfort of His disciples, because doing so went against social and religious norms. Jesus told these parables to get the attention of the Jewish listeners, and he got my attention as well.

Whether different in color, nationality, economic status, or creed, let's drop our prejudices and begin to ask God how we can love the strangers in front of us.

Ask Yourself...

Are there immigrants or refugees in my city? Do I know any of them?

Research and consider ways you and your family can help.

_____

_____

There are international students at almost every university. Organizations like ISM, ISI, Navigators, and Intervarsity are always looking for families to offer hospitality to these students.

Can I help out even once?

_____

_____

Will I ask God to open my heart to be hospitable in some way? What did God ask me to do?

_____

_____

Dig Deeper...

Read the story Jesus told of the Good Samaritan in Luke 10:25-37 and of His encounter with the Samaritan woman at the well in John 4:4-30.

How do both stories illustrate the power of loving a stranger from a different background?

_____

_____

How did Jesus highlight the hospitality and humanity of the Samaritans above His Jewish listeners to get their attention?

_____

_____

Did Jesus get your attention as He did mine?

_____

_____

Note: As defined by U.S. law and the 1951 Refugee Convention, refugees are migrants seeking entry from a third country who are able to demonstrate that they have been persecuted, or have reason to fear persecution, based on one of five "protected grounds": race, religion, nationality, political opinion, or membership in a particular social group. According to the UN refugee agency, there were nearly twenty-seven million refugees worldwide as of mid-2022, almost half of whom came from just two countries: Syria and Ukraine.[7]

Asylum seekers are those who meet the criteria for refugee status but apply from within the United States or at ports of entry after arriving under a different status.

---

[7] https://www.cfr.org/backgrounder/how-does-us-refugee-sys-tem-work-trump-biden-afghanistan#:~:text=How%20many%20 refugees%20are%20allowed,1980%20to%202025%2C465%20 in%202022.

Asylum seekers follow a different protocol than those applying for refugee status.

Immigrant visas are issued to foreign nationals who intend to live permanently in the United States. Nonimmigrant visas are for foreign nationals wishing to enter the United States temporarily - for tourism, medical treatment, business, temporary work, study, or other similar reasons.

At my father's funeral, dozens of people approached me and my siblings with the same message, "I think I was one of his favorite people and he was one of mine." We laughed because we knew it was true. He valued everyone he knew and wanted to get to know everyone he met. – Anne McCune

"Start children off on the way they should go, and even when they are old they will not turn from it." Proverbs 22:6 (NIV)

CHAPTER 8

Nurturing Hospitality at Home

Growing up, I lived in a large drafty home on the shores of Lake Erie, south of Buffalo, NY, in a little town called Lake View. We lived next door to my mother's parents. One set of first cousins lived on the opposite side of Grandma's house and the other set lived five houses down to our right. Grandma's door was always open, as was ours, and the doors to the cousins' houses. There was a lot of traffic between the houses.

One summer, our grandparents bought a trampoline for all the grandkids and since our house was central, it got placed in our yard. We became a hub for the whole neighborhood. Kids were always coming and going, jumping on the trampoline, and playing kickball in the yard. Most of them we knew, some we didn't, but all were welcome.

On Memorial Day, the Fourth of July, and Labor Day the families rotated hosting a picnic. My grandmother would get out a big turkey roasting pan and make pounds of potato salad, transfer it to bowls, and then make over fifty hamburger patties to go with the dozens of hotdogs. As a kid, it seemed like there were always more strangers than family who showed up, but I was told to be kind and friendly to all.

Easter, Thanksgiving, and Christmas celebrations were also large gatherings, although for these indoor events, numbers were usually limited to forty or so. We were a large Catholic family. There was always a celebration going on, either a birthday, Christening, First Communion, Confirmation, Wedding, or Funeral.

Life was lived in community. Friends and work acquaintances with nowhere else to go were always welcome. Gatherings were never perfect, but there was always plenty of food, drink, music, and games. There were people old and young and every age in between. Perhaps that is one reason why hospitality has always come easily to me.

Another reason was my dad. At 6'4'' and 240 pounds, my dad was a big man with twinkly eyes, a big laugh, and a great sense of humor. He was the head of the sales department for the family business, a printing company my mother's father and his brother started during the Depression. My dad studied hard to be a better salesman and he passed on some of the lessons to us kids. He taught us how to look people in the eye, give a firm handshake, and answer the phone politely, always giving our names ("Vogt's residence...Annie speaking").

He was always bringing home guests unexpectedly. My mother was easygoing and never fussed over meals. She had a great knack for throwing lavish impromptu meals together at the last minute.

Often before and after dinner, my dad would have us play cards with his elderly aunts and other people whom he invited to the house. Even though I can still hear him saying, "Children should be seen and not heard!" it was always said in a joking way where we knew we were welcome to be part of the conversation. He had a way of making everyone feel at home and at ease.

This confidence of loving strangers came with me into my college, young adult years, and into my marriage.

Hosting people in our home was something Lee and I have done since we were first married. Our college church believed in fellowship which included sharing meals and sharing life in a way similar to the young churches found in the New Testament scriptures. Lee and I attended the same church in our college years. We heard the same messages, saw the same fruit of those living that way, and determined to be generous and hospitable as a newly married couple.

We lived in married student housing at Dartmouth during medical school. Then, we moved to Lancaster, PA, for Lee's residency in Family Practice medicine. It was interesting to live among the Amish and Mennonite communities in Southern Pennsylvania. They practice hospitality within their communities, but many of their cultural norms forbid them from extending close hospitality to those outside their communities.

The resident-in-training doctors at Lancaster General Hospital and the Quarryville Community Health Center were encouraged by the head of the residency program, Dr. Nick Zervanos, to form a tight community. Dr. Zervanos was Greek, and there was a strong Greek community in Lancaster as well as strong Hispanic communities. Newcomers to the area from any of these unique communities were all easily absorbed and made to feel at home. The residents that were part of Lee's program included both single and newly married men and women. The physicians worked grueling schedules, being on call every third night, and all day most days with few days off, and little time to make friends outside of the hospital.

We started hosting Bible studies for both the residents and their spouses in our home. This aided in helping form strong friendships during those stressful years.

One Easter, I invited about a dozen of them to celebrate Easter brunch with us. We had a tiny home. We extended the table with card tables and folding chairs. Though I had not cooked for a large group by myself before, I was excited to be feeding so many people, especially the single men who seemed eager for a home-cooked meal.

We said grace and sat down. My husband started to carve the ham and noticed a problem. We soon realized what I thought was a pre-cooked ham just needing to be warmed up, was actually a fresh ham needing at least four more hours of cooking to be edible. The men groaned. They were hungry. Soon everyone was on their feet making peanut butter sandwiches, cutting cheese to eat with crackers, making bowls of cereal and milk, and basically eating everything edible they could find in our house.

Meanwhile, the ham went back in the oven, and we promised them dinner in a few hours. Some stayed and played games. Others went for hikes and came back for dinner. When they all returned, we sat together for a second meal to celebrate the Resurrection. It was an Easter we remember, not for the fine food, but for the fellowship. My mistake and vulnerability made others feel more at ease and even more welcome into our lives and homes.

When we moved to Syracuse, NY, for the public health payback period of Lee's medical school scholarship, my parents provided a bridge loan so we could close on a house in the city with a small third-floor bed and bathroom. Then they happened to mention the loan came with a small caveat. They had been talking to friends of theirs whose son Kurt had just graduated from college and landed a job in Syracuse. They told the parents Kurt could live with us until he found a place of his own.

We had a two-year-old and one on the way. We were a bit nervous about how our lifestyle and Kurt's would mesh.

111

As it turned out, it was great for the few months he stayed with us. Kurt was respectful of us, and we were of him. It was a learning experience to be sure, but it stretched us and helped us see if we had room to spare, God was going to fill it up.

After Kurt moved out, the room was empty for a few months. Then Obi moved in. Obi was a Nigerian doctor working at the same inner-city clinic where Lee worked. His wife and children had not yet arrived in the country, and he needed a place to live for a few months. We welcomed him to stay with us, and then discovered that he smoked! If you are a non-smoker like we were, you can imagine how this might have been a problem, especially since our household now included a new baby girl. It's not an unforgivable habit, but I was a bit grumpy dealing with unwanted smoke and smells in our house. We were able to talk honestly with Obi and worked out solutions so we could both live comfortably under the same roof. It was another good lesson in our learning curve on loving strangers. We remained in touch with Obi and his family throughout the years.

> *Good communication is essential to maintain a non-grumbling, hospitable heart.*

We made a conscious effort to get to know our neighbors and community in Syracuse. Our church met on Sundays in the chapel at the local rescue mission where one of the pastors worked full time. All three pastors had full-time jobs outside of the church. We learned so much from them. The first Sunday we attended, the lead pastor asked us to come to lunch at his house the following week after church. Deciding I should bring something, I made a small pan of brownies. However, I was embarrassed to find out they had ten children. The pastor's wife took my meager offering with great graciousness and a twinkle in her eye. The second week, another pastor asked us to come to his house after services the following week. This time I asked how big his family was and planned accordingly! Everyone at the church welcomed strangers and newcomers with graciousness and ease including the many men and women from the mission who attended.

We talked a lot about hospitality at home with our growing family. We had a mailman who walked the streets and delivered our mail to the slot by our front door. Our three-year-old son Dave was excited to see the mailman come each day. On several occasions, he begged him to come inside and have lunch with us. We tried to explain the mailman still had work to do without dampening David's enthusiasm for offering hospitality to strangers!

Soon, we were moving to Orchard Park, NY, with three little ones. We determined as best as possible to always make sure there was a room we could quickly convert to a guest room, even if it meant reassigning kids to other spaces for a while. We asked the pastor of our new church to come and give a blessing over our house so we might welcome many through our doors. We again got to know our neighbors and made friends at church, school, and through Lee's work in the community.

We had fun hosting neighborhood groups, backyard vacation clubs, and lots of other gatherings. Friends and family visited for dinner and overnight stays. We also had some interesting strangers, like four young women from around the state who were competing in a Junior Miss Pageant. Every time I turned around, each was in need of something that was new territory for me. Could I help with her gymnastic routine? Costumes? Makeup? Words of encouragement were needed to calm the nerves of these ambitious and competitive young adults.

Shortly after giving birth to our 4th child, we came into an unexpected inheritance. This allowed us to move one street over to a larger house where we could host even more guests.

Our family of six also started taking medical mission trips to Honduras to work with missionaries there from our church. On the last day of our first trip, through unusual circumstances, we met a 4-year-old girl named Suany who lived in a small village near the rainforest. Suany needed surgery for a congenital heart defect. The little girl was so weak she could barely walk. Her lungs were overworked from breathing in wood smoke from their adobe stove while trying to compensate for her weak heart. We were told her life expectancy was quite short unless she had open heart surgery, but there were no pediatric heart surgeons in the country at that time.

Sonia, Suany's mother, had been praying that God would send someone who could take her to the USA for the needed surgery. She looked at us with pleading eyes. Our hearts were touched by these strangers. My husband was a family physician, not a surgeon, so we prayed with them and hoped for a miracle. Maybe God would heal her right there.

But the miracle came in ways we did not expect, and within a few months, Suany and her mother Sonia were able to fly to our house with a translator. A surgeon at Children's Hospital in Buffalo agreed to do the surgery pro bono. Friends and family helped with airfare and hospital costs. Neither Sonya nor Suany had ever been on an airplane, let alone in a house with indoor plumbing. Sonia stood at the sink and stared as she was able to turn it on and off. They delighted in hot showers, bathtubs, and our washing machine. Thankfully, the delicate open heart surgery was successful, and she healed quickly and recovered fully.

Suany and Sonia lived with us for 6 weeks, which included Christmas. We were humbled to recognize the excess we usually spent on the holiday while hosting these precious strangers who came from such poverty. They were gracious and grateful for anything we were able to offer them. Two days before Christmas our youngest son Mark had an asthma attack which landed him in the same hospital where Suany was recovering. We realized tearfully, that if we had lived on the mountaintop in Honduras, our son would not have made it to medical care in time. This incident tendered our hearts as a family to be open to whomever God might bring our way in the future.

We continued to offer love to strangers in other countries by bringing medical teams to Honduras for the next 3 decades. These trips also allowed us to visit Sonia and Suany up in the mountain village, and to watch Suany grow up, live a normal life, and become the mother of three healthy children.

Back in Orchard Park, our reputation for hospitality was growing. The secretary of our elementary school, Mrs. T, was a lovely woman with roots in Eastern Europe who sang in a choir. It was an important part of her life. Though I had sung with several choirs and singing groups in high school and college, I had no idea choral singing was such an important pastime. The choralsinging.org website boasts over 57 million Americans are part of choral groups singing in concert halls, places of worship, schools, and on street corners, all for the joy of singing together. They travel around the country and the world.

Choirs from around the globe travel on cultural exchanges. Most of them are not professional singers. They can barely afford the transportation expenses and often rely on the hospitality of the "home choirs" to find places to house and feed them as well as places for them to sing. Wherever you live there are probably several choirs singing somewhere this week and many are staying in host family homes.

One day as I was having copies of the PTO newsletter made in the school office, I asked Mrs. T how her day was going.

"Not well," she said. "I need to find places to house several choir members who are coming from Lithuania to put on a concert this weekend. Would you be interested in helping?"

"Sure, we would love to," I answered.

We had housed a teacher from Japan on a two-month exchange several months earlier. We hosted four lovely women from Lithuania who taught us how to make the strongest coffee we had ever seen (it was way too thick for us to even try drinking it, though). We learned so much about how hard and bleak life was in Eastern Europe. Singing and traveling with the choir was a high point in their weeks and their lives. The concert was magnificent. It was obvious what an important place music played in their ability to cope with the other hardships in their lives. Their travels would not have been possible without Americans opening their homes to them to offset the other costs. We were honored to help out.

A year later, Mrs. T caught me in the school hallway. She had a Polish boys' choir coming and asked if I could take some of the boys overnight. Of course, we did. We attended the concert. The singing from these young and pure voices was inspiring. My kids were already in bed by the time the two young men who were staying with us arrived at our home. We showed them to their rooms, and we all went to sleep. In the morning, I asked my boys to tell our guests to come to breakfast.

"How?" they asked. "They only speak Polish, and we only speak English!"

We practiced some charade moves like eating from a bowl, drinking from a cup, and motioning to follow so they might help the Polish boys find their way to the kitchen. My boys were a little nervous, but I told them the other boys were probably more nervous. Soon, I had the boys from both nations eating cereal, smiling, laughing, and communicating in ways they could all understand. Chris brought out a soccer ball and motioned to go outside. The boys had a great morning and played until their rides came to pick them up and get them to the next stop on their concert itinerary. We took lots of pictures of the boys hugging and smiling. My children were the key to the warm welcome.

> **Loving strangers is rewarding at any age.**

Next came the African children's choir. Our church was the sponsoring agency and the concert was going to take place in the sanctuary. We housed several kids and their "Aunties" who traveled with them and taught them while they were on the road. We took them to swim at my cousin's pool. The joy on their faces was irrepressible. My hospitable cousin, Mary Clare, lived down the street, had several children of her own, and never got tired of me showing love to the strangers we brought her way while we hosted them.

The word seemed to have gotten out, and there were frequent calls to host. The strangers came in pairs, fours, or whole teams like the Scottish boys' soccer team that was in town for a tournament. We had four members of a girl's swim team from N.H. stay a week. A Northwestern University Spring break group of nine (mostly international students who couldn't go home for the break) stayed when passing through on their way to Boston. We hosted Chinese and Pakistani International students from Penn State, Young Life youth groups traveling across the state, missionaries from India, Teen Challenge leaders from several states with groups of teenagers, Glee club singers, the ultimate frisbee team from Dartmouth, and the ballet troupe I already mentioned. We hosted a young man from Japan who was on a student teaching exchange at our elementary school. While raising four young children, limiting our ability to travel, the world was coming to us!

As the years sped by, our kids made friends from around the country. Somehow our town seemed to be on the way to or from wherever their friends were going. Hospitality became a lifestyle for our family. Everyone helped, and the help of everyone is what made it work. Rarely would a month go by when we were not hosting someone extra. One weekend my oldest son, who was living in another state at the time, came home unexpectedly for a visit. He came down to breakfast to find another young man helping himself to a bowl of cereal. As they sat at the counter Paul introduced himself and asked my son who he was. Dave answered and said "This is my house" who are you? Paul answered, "I live here too!" Paul was a Young Life leader working at our high school who had gotten tired of dorm life at the college he was attending and moved in with us. They both laughed. We had gotten so used to people coming and going we often forgot to alert our grown kids when there were new residents at the house. We had the privilege of meeting and showing love to many strangers over the years, and we were all greatly enriched by it.

Our neighbors wondered if we had some secret sign on our roof that said, "Strangers welcome here." My mother-in-law often joked that the "no-vacancy" sign at the entrance to our street was never turned on.

No sign was needed. Word spread. We were the lucky ones to have a reputation for having a ready welcome for all and to be able to meet so many wonderful people. Our children learned, as I had, that there is great joy to be found in a hospitable home. All four of them now have homes of their own where there is rarely an empty bed. They are teaching their children the blessing of practicing hospitality. Hospitality can be caught as well as taught. Wouldn't it be wonderful if the next generation could catch it from you and me, and play it forward?

My hope is if you have not had an opportunity yet, you will begin to make space in your heart and home. God knows, sees, and sends the strangers in need of love (and or lodging if you have room) to your door. Make your whole family a part of the welcome crew.

Ask Yourself...

Have I begun to make space in my heart and home to serve God by extending love and lodging to the strangers God sends to my door?

_____

_____

Are there any examples I have from growing up of extending hospitality to strangers?

_____

_____

What have I learned from this chapter to help me make others feel welcome in my home?

_____

_____

Dig Deeper...

Our college church believed in fellowship which included sharing meals and sharing life like the young churches found in the New Testament.

Read Acts 9:13-10:48.

Record what you learn from these verses.

_____

_____

_____

_____

Read the following verses from Romans 12:13-20 describing how New Testament Christian churches developed fellowships. **Record** what you learn from each verse.

Verse 13

_____

_____

Verse 14

_____

_____

Verse 15

_____

_____

Verse 16 & 17

_____

_____

Verse 18 & 19

_____

_____

Verse 20

_____

_____

"I was sick and you tended to my needs..."
(Matthew 25:36 VOICE)

The words *hospital* and *hospice* had their origin in the concept of *hospitality*.

CHAPTER 9

The Recovery Room

"Honor your father and mother"—which is the first
commandment with a promise, "so that it may go well
with you and that you may enjoy long life on the earth."
(Ephesians 6:3 and Deuteronomy 5:16 NIV)

We always tried to make space for our parents when they came to visit, be it a short weekend, or a prolonged stay. The house in Orchard Park had four bedrooms, all upstairs, when we moved in with our four children. It also had a large unfinished basement. Within months of moving in, we decided to finish the basement and include a bedroom and bathroom for parents and other visitors.

We thought it was a great setup so Lee's parents would be comfortable when they would come for several weeks each fall. A few years into their yearly visits, I saw my father-in-law standing on the first-floor stairwell, looking down at the flight of steps that would take him to his room. He was obviously thinking about going down, but was hesitant for some reason. He was hobbling a bit, but it hadn't dawned on me he had severe arthritis pain, and navigating the steps was an issue for him. If he had forgotten a sweater, or book, or anything else, he was forced to decide between his need for it and the pain of retrieving the item. He was in his early eighties. He was a military man and a servant-hearted gentleman, who could not bring himself to ask me to run down and get something for him. There was an embarrassment of losing the ability to do things for himself. When I asked if I could help, he just shook his head and walked away.

Later, I related the incident to Lee, and we decided we needed to figure out how to make a handicapped-accessible bedroom in our home that his parents could use for their future visits. I realize that making space is not feasible for most of you reading this, so my encouragement is not necessarily to do what we did, but to consider those who brought you up, physically and spiritually, and pray how to bless them as they approach the end of life. We experienced an overflow of grace for each effort we made, and I am convinced you will, too. We knew the first-floor guest room we envisioned would be a costly stretch for us. What we didn't know then, was how God was planning to use that room to bless so many people in addition to our parents, for the remaining twenty years we lived in that house.

"Build it and they will come," is a line from the classic film *"Field of Dreams."* It proved all too true in our case. Our new room quickly got nicknamed "The Recovery Room." Within weeks of completion, both Lee's parents and mine were scheduling the hip and knee replacements they had been putting off, and asking if they could spend their rehab weeks with us. It was a bonus for them that Lee was a geriatric physician and could be a comforting professional resource during their recoveries. Our four kids were old enough to be pleasant company and able to help whenever needed. My part was to intentionally be available to organize meals, visitors, transportation, and companionship.

A year after my mother (age 70) passed away, my father (age 77) re-married a wonderful woman named Pam. They booked the recovery room for a few weeks while he was having a knee replacement. Pam was quite a good sport as she got used to our open-door policy. One evening I found her in the back hallway counting shoes. It was a night when Young Life was meeting in our family room. There were over 60 pairs of smelly teenager shoes lined up!

Another morning we had gone out early. Pam woke up to find there was a "clown in the kitchen" making breakfast! The night before, we had mentioned to her and Dad that we had overnight guests coming who would be staying in the lower-level guestroom. But we forgot to tell Pam that this man was a professional clown who was part of a ministry team. He would dress in makeup and costume before he had breakfast and headed out the door. If I had known earlier, I would have prepared my dad and Pam. Fortunately, Dad had always been a big fan of circuses and clowns. We all had a good laugh. Lee and I learned to be better at communicating and preparing all houseguests for possible surprises that come with a hospitable house.

When our parents weren't there for rehab or to visit, other friends occasionally called and booked the recovery room. One had just had minor surgery and needed a few days of rest with no driving. Another was having kidney stones removed. They were invited to rest for a few days at our place. In between those visits, we offered the room to out-of-town guests who were thankfully quite healthy, and always enjoyed the beautiful views of the woods and woodland creatures behind our house.

We were privileged to host missionaries from India, Africa, Honduras, and Albania, among other countries, not to mention many from across America. Jesus said in Matthew 10 when His disciples came to a town and "worthy persons" took them in to stay, there would be a blessing for those hosts and their homes. We feel we have received such a blessing time and time again.

As many of you know, taking on elder care tests the extent of our capacity for hospitality physically and emotionally. God's Word tells us to offer hospitality to one another without grumbling (1 Peter 4:9). This reminder was an important spiritual realignment for me when I was overwhelmed and grumbling on the inside. There was a several-month period where both of our fathers needed extra help. It coincided with our middle son dealing with cancer and our daughter needing delicate surgery.

My dad was suffering from Alzheimer's and needed round-the-clock care. While we waited for an opening at a memory care facility near our home, my stepmom asked if they could stay in the recovery room. After several weeks, a room opened for him at a wonderful memory care unit. We were given the go-ahead to move some furniture in. He was to be admitted a few days later when all the paperwork was cleared.

Then came the fall. My dad was a big man. We were out doing errands when we got the call from my petite stepmom. Dad had fallen and she had called the EMT squad to help him get up since he had wedged himself in a doorway when he fell. He had pain in his arm and was disoriented so they took him immediately to the hospital. He had broken his shoulder. Due to his injury and his inability to "transfer from chair to standing or bed" without assistance, he no longer qualified for the memory care unit at the facility. He would have to wait for a bed on the skilled care floor to open. It could be a few days or weeks. He needed rehab and was temporarily moved to a nursing home where my husband worked.

Within days of my dad being at the nursing home, Lee's mom called from Florida. She was driving north with his dad who had suddenly taken a turn for the worse health-wise. She would be there in 24 hours and asked if the recovery room was ready. I barely had time to clear out my dad's things and reset the room for Lee's mom and dad. My father-in-law was now eighty-nine years old and suffering from a type of lymphoma requiring increasingly frequent blood transfusions. It became clear they would not be going back to Florida. Our home was to become his hospice care center.

Hospice care is a very special category of hospitality.

Lee's dad was not a stranger who needed our love. He was well-known and loved by all of us. However, he and my mother-in-law were experiencing a new strange, and scary reality as they faced death head-on. Only God knows the days or hours we have left. Hospice doctors I have spoken to say they give estimates but humbly admit they are often wrong. Hospice care traditionally starts when a patient is diagnosed with less than six months to live. Thankfully, hospice is not only about dying well, but also about living those last months as well as possible, physically, mentally, emotionally, and spiritually.

Our home now required making space in the recovery room (eventually for a hospital bed), space in the rest of the house for visitors and healthcare workers, and more space in our schedules, heads, and hearts. Both mom and dad needed extra time and care. Ironically, just before his dad arrived in June, my husband had signed up to take a rigorous exam certifying him in Hospice care. The exam was scheduled for late September. It required him to study 2-3 hours a night on top of his day job and time with his family and his mom and dad. He passed the test, but his dad passed into heaven less than a month later leaving much of the work caring for his dad and mom to me.

My responsibilities at the time also included being part of the care team with my stepmom and sisters committed to making sure my dad had daily visitors. This care was both at the nursing home where he rehabbed the broken shoulder and later at the skilled care facility where he would spend his last 19 months. The transitions were taxing on him and the whole family, which is often the case for the elderly. It was a difficult season all around. We were thrown into learning new ways of loving family and strangers.

Hospice care involves loving lots of strangers besides the patient. For patients with dementia, it is quite common for them to no longer recognize family. We become strangers to them. Even for patients with clear minds like my father-in-law, each day brought an assortment of new care-team people to our home including nurses, aides, therapists, and ministers. Friends and family stopped by. Meals occasionally arrived from various sources. Believe me, every kindness and meal was gratefully received! While we tried to create a peaceful and serene environment for Lee's dad, and my dad, the days were often intense for everyone.

The amazing thing is that every ounce of our effort seemed to be met with an invisible grace from God. While we were all seemingly depleted, we were also being filled up in intangible ways. There were sweet days filled with memories, laughter, and joy. There were also bittersweet days of fear, tears, and angst as we watched both my dad's and my father-in-law's mortal bodies slow down. Grief crept in as they both wrestled with the loss of the ability to care for themselves.

Finally, the day came, first for Lee's dad, and then for mine, where the veil between heaven and earth became thin. They took that last breath as the bodies that had held them here released their souls to heaven. An astonishing peace prevailed. As Christians, we have the confidence to know that life on earth is only a small fraction of the life that God has promised us. God is good. All the time. Even at the end of life here. Their lives, so well lived on earth, began anew, free from sickness and pain.

D.L. Moody, a Christian publisher from the late 1800s, said concerning that transition, "At that moment I shall be more alive than I am now; I shall have gone up higher, that is all, out of this old clay tenement into a house that is immortal-a body that death cannot touch, that sin cannot taint."[8] That moment of death comes to all of us and is not to be feared if we have put our trust in Christ. If you are reading this and have no idea what I am

---

[8]   Dwight L. Moody (2017). "Secret Power: The Secret of Success in Christian Life and Work", p.75, Aneko Press

talking about, I pray that you will pursue any curiosity and ask a Christian friend or God himself to help you face any fear you may have. As you read earlier in this book, God is always listening and often answers in ways more clearly than we expect.

Many people have opened their homes to provide hospice care to family members in their final days. My neighbor took in family friends from another state during COVID so the husband could get better treatment at the Cancer Center nearby rather than face a nine-hour drive each time he needed treatment. They stayed for nine months.

Another friend insisted her mother-in-law, Jean, come to their home during her final months. She readied a room for Jean by repainting the walls in her mother-in-law's favorite color. She set up an art studio for Jean to be able to continue to do the things that brought her joy. My friend welcomed her sisters-in-law and family to come and stay and visit whenever and for as long as they wanted to. Not because she had the space or capacity, but because she was willing to make the space.

> *It is a difficult and sometimes uncomfortable privilege to offer this kind of hospitality. It is not an easy season no matter how long it lasts. Yet, every day is precious.*

Taking on hospice care in your home should not be entered into lightly. Like adoption and foster care, it requires making sure everyone in the household agrees with taking on this degree of hospitality. Everyone needs to be able to make the emotional space for the patient to be cared for and loved well by all. There are other places where hospice care can take place: nursing homes, hospice centers, hospitals, and the patient's own home. These are valid options to be considered. My dad passed away at the skilled care facility where he lived for 19 months. The staff became like family as we got to know them and we showed our appreciation for the care they provided my dad when we were not there. We could not have managed his 24-hour needs at our home as well as they were able to.

For those who can make space and take the risk, I hope you find as I did, the mystical grace God wrapped us in during that season. God sustained us in ways we could never have imagined. Others who have entered this realm of hospitality have told me the same thing. They feel a grace they cannot explain. God cares for the vulnerable in far greater measure than we can know or imagine. He equips us to pass on His love in tangible ways to those who need it most even when we doubt our own strength to do it.

King Solomon reminds us, "Because of the Lord's great love, we are not consumed, for his compassions never fail. They are new every morning. Great is your faithfulness!" (Lamentations 3:22-23 NIV). Words of hope like these turned my grumbling heart into one of thankfulness and gave me the strength to persevere.

That season now reminds me of my ability to support families going through a similar season whether their loved one is at their home, or elsewhere. I can send flowers, fruit, meals, puzzles, or small gifts. It was during this season I learned to enjoy doing crossword puzzles as my sisters and husband would work on them together with me while tending to my dad's care. It is therapeutic to feel like you have accomplished something when so much of the rest of your days are spent dealing with the unknown.

Visits from those who loved us and our dads were a huge blessing. We all enjoyed the hours when friends with musical talents would come and share their gifts in our home. Our dads felt buoyed by the respect, dignity, and sincere love given so freely by others. We did, too.

For those hosting a season of hospice, the hours, days, and months spent loving our loved ones may become some of our most precious times and memories. My hope is that more of us will take the risk of opening our own homes and practicing hospice-style hospitality. We can be renewed in our love and hospitality towards those going through such a vulnerable season whenever and wherever that may be.

The words hospital and hospice had their origin in the concept of hospitality. The first hospices took care of pilgrims who needed rest and restoration on their long journeys. We can do the same for those needing our care at the end of their life journeys. It is a beautiful way to honor our parents and support others traveling on that road.

Ask Yourself...

Does being around people with dementia or serious illness bother me? Why or why not?

_____

_____

Declare: I will pray about overcoming my fears to be available to those who may need my love.

Is it time for me to speak about end-of-life issues together with my family?

_____

_____

End-of-life issues can be a difficult but helpful conversation.

How can I make space physically or timewise for the ill and vulnerable, or to help those helping them?

_____

_____

Dig Deeper...

Read the following scriptures and record what you learn about how Jesus helped those who were dealing with serious illness and the potential death of themselves or a loved one.

Matthew 10:11-15 –

_____

_____

Luke 8:40-56

_____

_____

Matthew 25:31-46

_____

_____

Romans 12:9 says, "Love must be sincere." (NIV)

"Love from the center of who you are; don't fake it." (MSG)

CHAPTER 10

The Hospitality Industry

Hospitality has become one of the fastest-growing industries in the world. Globally the market was valued at $4,107 billion in 2022 and projected to grow to $9,950 billion by 2028.[9] That is a lot of money spent by people seeking food, lodging, travel, and entertainment. People love to be served and serviced. Companies engaging in this market want to connect with their customers and they want them to return. Customer loyalty is not randomly generated. It can be achieved by paying attention to several factors. Many of these factors have become known as "Rules of Hospitality."

A quick search on the internet will provide you with several lists of market-oriented "Rules of Hospitality." These rules and instructions originated with the hospitality

---

[9] https://www.marketdataforecast.com/market-reports/the-state-of-the-hospitality-market

industry, but they have also become cornerstones of training for other businesses that depend on customer satisfaction and service.

Gabby Ott works at a Sheraton Resort in Colorado. On a warm Tuesday afternoon, she was dressed in Western gear and welcoming me and others in the lobby of the hotel, offering free beverages and engaging verbally as I approached to get my cup of lemonade. When she asked me why I was visiting, I told her my main reason for being there was to take time to work on this book. She allowed me to ask her a lot of questions about hospitality and the training she had received. She told me about the 15/10/5 rule which she was taught early on in her training as a resort's activities manager.

It goes something like this:

> ➤ Pay attention if you spot a guest approaching 15 feet away. If you are engaged in another activity or a conversation with another staff member, be prepared to disengage.
>
> ➤ If the guest comes within 10 feet, make eye contact and smile.
>
> ➤ If they come within 5 feet, offer a kind greeting as you continue to smile. Introduce yourself and ask how you can serve them.

Some industries shorten this to just the 10/5 rule. The essential part is smiling, making eye contact, and venturing to speak when a guest/customer/stranger is near enough to connect with. You probably have been greeted with a smile because of this rule whether at a hotel, restaurant, or other business. (Think car dealership!)

Healthcare establishments like hospitals and nursing homes have also found the Hospitality Rules healthful as well as helpful to both staff, clients, and their bottom line. I found this article on a healthcare website:

> "Human beings are hardwired to read each other's faces to identify how they are feeling. This helps us act appropriately towards the other person. As explained in Neuroscience News, 'an instinct for facial mimicry allows us to empathize with and even experience other people's feelings.' As humans working in such a compassionate field as healthcare, empathy can wreak havoc on us and others with whom we associate. The last thing we want to do is spread one person's sadness to another. The good news is that we can reset our emotions with a smile.

Research shows that contracting your facial muscles to smile causes more blood to flow to your frontal lobes and causes your brain to release the same mood-enhancing chemical as coffee, chocolate, and even cocaine—dopamine. So, you're happy because you smile, and you smile because you are happy. It's like a loop. What's more, research shows that it doesn't matter if you are faking the smile, the brain still produces dopamine. So, it even works to 'fake it until you make it'.

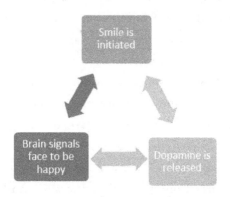

Ochsner Health System in Louisiana decided to use this knowledge to educate and train the entire staff to smile whenever they were within ten feet and say, "Hello," any time they were within five feet of another person, whether that person was a patient or staff member. They didn't simply send a memo, hang a sign or two, and forget about it. They practiced the rule, and it became so natural that staff felt awkward if they didn't smile and greet each other and patients. It's no coincidence that in 2015, Ochsner Health System's operating surplus grew 429%."[10]

Who knew that smiling and offering hospitality has measurable financial benefits in some sectors?

Living in the Atlanta area, I have seen the effect hospitality training by one company has had on an entire city. If you have ever been to a Chick-fil-A restaurant or drive-thru and said, "Thank you" to someone who serves you, you will be immediately responded to with a smile and the phrase, "My pleasure."

The story behind this is that Truett Cathy, the founder of Chick-fil-A, first heard the phrase used by employees at a Ritz-Carlton. He mentioned it at his company's annual

---

[10] https://www.icontracts.com/
how-to-implement-the-10-and-5-rule-in-nursing-homes/

seminar for franchise owners in 2001, suggesting that even if Chick-fil-A was not on the level of a 5-star hotel chain, the gracious pleasantry might be a nice way to distinguish the service at their fast-food restaurants.

According to Steve Robinson, Chick-fil-A's former longtime marketing chief, in his book "Covert Cows and Chick-fil-A," it wasn't until 2003—when Cathy's son Dan, who later became CEO, started saying "my pleasure" himself and pushing others to follow suit—that it became an unwritten rule at the company, as it remains today.

"It dawned on me that this could be a service signature for us, almost like two pickles on a sandwich," Dan Cathy said.

Chick-fil-A leaders tapped a marketing executive to overhaul its entire service strategy, which grew to include training workers to greet customers with a smile, make eye contact, and speak in an enthusiastic voice."[11]

When I heard the phrase used almost daily everywhere I went in Atlanta, I wondered if it was because so many people had worked at and been trained by Chick-fil-A, which has many restaurants here. Now, I think it is because so many people here in Atlanta have been greeted and responded to at Chick-fil-A restaurants that it has become a contagious phrase.

Other rules of hospitality include anticipating needs, listening attentively, and serving graciously. We can learn

---

[11] https://www.cnn.com/2022/04/09/business/chick-fil-a-my-pleasure/index.html

from the hospitality industry, and even more importantly, improve on it. They appear to "love strangers" well. As Christians, we can offer hospitality in the form of a smile and simple greeting almost all the time. Not because we are being paid to do so, or for the financial gain of our employers, but because it reflects the love God has for every human being, and it yields lasting rewards.

Unlike the article on healthcare I quoted, we shouldn't have to "fake it till we make it." When we remember how fully loved we are, it becomes a sincere motivation to use those facial muscles and spread some kindness and joy. Philippians 2:4 says, "Let each of you look not only to his own interests, but also to the interests of others" (ESV). It is a reminder I often need to be more attentive to the needs of those around me as I try to practice hospitality.

Though I am glad the hospitality industry is thriving, genuine hospitality should be thriving, too. Every time I read the story in Luke where Mary and Joseph were turned away from the inn because there was no room, I am saddened to think how our Lord came into the world lacking basic hospitality. I remember my experience on a study tour in Israel when we were in a cave where sheep had slept the night before. It was not as cute as the pictures of our nativity make it out to be. The cave where Mary, Joseph, and baby Jesus slept was probably as smelly and dirty as the one we visited.

While I am sad that the innkeeper could not accommodate the family in need, I am glad that some space was made available. There should be rooms available in our homes even when the inns around us are full, and we should not be embarrassed to offer whatever humble space we have for God.

There is a Motel company that advertises "We'll leave the light on for you." My prayer, whether or not Motel 6 has left a light on, is that I too will leave a light on and be ready to welcome those whom Christ sends to my door. When they come, I will smile and welcome them in.

Ask Yourself...

What have I appreciated most about the hotels I have stayed at?

_____

_____

What besides good food makes for a good restaurant?

_____

_____

Have I ever tried the 10/5 rule?

_____

_____

Does my church have a hospitality team? Do they use the 10/5 rule?

_____

_____

Should everyone at church use it?

_____

_____

Jesus had His disciples prepare an upper room for the Passover.

What would be the equivalent today?

_____

_____

_____

Dig Deeper:

Read Luke 2.

What thoughts come to mind concerning hospitality?

_____

_____

Ponder these Proverbs:

> Proverbs 15:30 "A cheerful look brings joy to the heart; good news makes for good health (NLT)"

> Proverbs 17:22 "A cheerful look is good medicine, but a broken spirit saps a person's strength (NLT)"

> **Read** the story of Elijah and the widow at Zarephath in 1 Kings 17:8-24.

> *What impressed you about this story?*

_____

_____

Read the story of Zacchaeus in Luke 19.

Would you be prepared if Jesus invited himself to your house?

_____

_____

So a church leader must be a man whose life is above reproach. He must be faithful to his wife. He must exercise self-control, live wisely, and have a good reputation. **He must enjoy having guests in his home,** *and he must be able to teach.*

(1 Timothy 3:2 NLT) ***Given to hospitality...*** (KJV emphasis added)

Every day they (the early followers) continued to meet together in the temple courts. **They broke bread in their homes** *and ate together with glad and sincere hearts, praising God and enjoying the favor of all the people. And the Lord added to their number daily those who were being saved.*

(Acts 2:46-47 NIV emphasis added)

CHAPTER 11

Christian

Hospitality at Church

While Lee was in residency in Lancaster, PA, a nurse named Ginger reached out and invited him and the other interns to join her at her church. It was called, Shalom Covenant Christian Fellowship and met in the lower level of a large farmhouse in a surrounding town. Many of the church attendees had made a covenant towards an intentional Christian Community. The elder of the small congregation lived at the farmhouse named Shalom along with his brother and his family, and several single women including Ginger.

After the Sunday service, the leader invited us all to stay for lunch. Immediately, everyone including the children were mobilized, setting tables, and helping to prepare a

Pennsylvania Dutch-style meal. We all sat together enjoying good food and delightful fellowship. It was hard not to want to return the following week when they invited us. The welcome was warm and sincere, and we felt a place of belonging. As a "Covenant Community," they were committed to sharing all things economically within the community, but also willing to give freely to those around them.

It soon became our church home for the rest of our three years of residency in Lancaster. We were not asked or required to "hold all things in common" the way most of the community had done up to that time. Yet, we learned a lot from their hospitality and generosity to each other and to us.

Our next church experience was in inner-city Syracuse, NY. The Federal government had placed us in a medically underserved area as a requirement for the Public Health scholarship that had paid Lee's medical school tuition. We began attending a non-denominational church which met at the Syracuse Rescue Mission. I wrote about some experiences there in a previous chapter.

Week after week, families from the church offered to welcome newcomers. This was a church that took hospitality seriously. We continued to learn a lot from this inner-city congregation about trusting God for provision and being the family of God to one another. Perhaps because of the weekly meetings at the rescue mission, along with Lee's medical work serving those in need, we appreciated being part of a church that practiced hospitality and was always on the lookout for loving strangers. It is one of the reasons we were more willing to open our own homes to those in need.

Our next move was to Western New York for the next thirty-six years. The Sunday School teacher at the first church we attended gave our kids such a warm welcome, that our children insisted we go back the next week. It was a much bigger congregation than we were used to, and although we didn't get weekly invitations to lunch (especially now that our family was growing), we found out the church hosted a lot of traveling groups and conferences. We joined the church and were soon asked to open our home to many people from all over the country and all over the world. It was a rich time of growth and learning for us.

The church itself was very hospitable. They frequently shared their facilities with other ministries and were always reaching out to those in need. Every summer, the lead pastor and his wife tried to have all the members over to their house in large groups on successive weeks. It was a beautiful gift of heartfelt hospitality that made members of the church feel loved and accepted like family. It was also a great example for all of us to follow.

Churches are expected to be hospitable. Many are, but sadly, many are not. It takes leadership and intentionality. It takes leaders who understand that loving strangers and taking care of both members and visitors is a mandatory requirement for leadership.

Trinity Anglican, the church I now attend in Atlanta, kicks off what they call "Team Sunday" every August. The staff all don sports jerseys of their choice as conversation starters, and dozens of "team members" (members of the congregation who sign up to help) gather to reinforce the vision of offering hospitality at church and "setting the table" for those who enter the doors of the church the rest of the year.

Among those in attendance are the various groups: hospitality and greeter team, the parking lot team, the childcare team, the communion serving team, the worship team, the prayer team, and the youth worker team. Each person on these teams works to create a welcoming environment for everyone who enters the doors of the church. The church prioritizes hospitality. Even for this meeting, individuals were greeted at the door and invited to sit at tables in the sanctuary (turned banquet room). Each table had a tray of cheese, crackers, and fruit on them. Cold water and carbonated water were served from large coolers. It was obvious some team members had already set a table for us before we entered the building.

Every person there felt the sweet Spirit of God dwelling among us. We felt loved and cared for. During a time of worship, the prayer team members weaved their way through the tables and prayed for each of us individually. We listened to words of encouragement, sang, and worshipped God together. Afterward, we split up around the building to meet with our individual teams to strategize best practices for welcoming and serving others throughout the new church year.

Our lead pastor made the point that the term "team members" was used intentionally. We are not just volunteers coming to the aid of a non-profit we support. The members of the church ARE the church.

When we all recognize that we are members belonging to one family, our churches become those places of welcome and grace in the very same way our individual homes should be. When the church does a good job at making every member feel loved, they can extend the love to all who come through the doors. Our hope for those who have never been to a church, or visited one recently, will by God's grace, and our efforts, feel loved and welcomed.

Everyone deserves to be accepted and welcomed as a child of God because that is what we all are!

The earliest gatherings of the church looked very different from most of our current weekend worship services. For the first 100 years or so, they included coming together for a meal and ending with the sacramental breaking of bread the way Jesus initiated it at the Last Supper. They called these "love feasts" or Agape meals. Historians say the apostles started this tradition in response to what Jesus asked them to do at the Last Supper. They were to remember Him as they ate broken bread and drank the blood of the covenant together.

The early disciples knew that one of the first times Jesus appeared after His resurrection, was during the breaking of bread with the travelers on the road to Emmaus. The twelve also experienced that soon after the resurrection when Jesus met His disciples on the beach and shared a meal of fish cooked over a fire. Perhaps after Jesus' ascension, they continued to meet over breaking bread with the hope Jesus would miraculously show up again as bread was broken and meals were shared.

The apostle Paul reminded the early Corinthian church, "For whenever you eat this bread and drink this cup, you proclaim the Lord's death until he comes" (I Corinthians 11:26 NIV).

> *They (the first followers) devoted themselves to the apostles' teaching and to fellowship, to the breaking of bread and to prayer.* Everyone was filled with awe at the many wonders and signs performed by the apostles. All the believers were together and had everything in common. They sold property and possessions to give to anyone who had need. Every day they continued to meet together in the temple courts. *They broke bread in their homes* and ate together with glad and sincere hearts, praising God and enjoying the favor of all the people. And the Lord added to their number daily those who were being saved. (Acts 2:42-47 NIV)

These fellowship meals eaten with gladness and sincerity of heart were intrinsic to their life together as

Christ followers. They were not a casual afterthought. The breaking of bread from house to house was an important part of their growing together as a united communal body. The sharing of their belongings with those in need and loving each new member of the gathering was one of the emblems of the new church. Hospitality toward each other was a worthy use of time and effort. It was a sign of obedience to God and love for His people. With new disciples being added daily, these shared meals and goods were a chance to fellowship, love the strangers among them, tell the stories of the miracles, and remind each other of the words and deeds of Christ. It was tangible evidence of the fulfillment of the ancient scriptures.

Unfortunately, by the end of the second century, the agape meal no longer had a central place in Christian tradition. The gatherings would include what we see today as the sacrament of communion, but the gatherings were more about teaching and prayer. These things are of course good and essential, but so was the fellowship time whose value seemed to be slipping away.

Even at its best, the agape meal was often tainted with abuses. The early church records some of these for us in the Book of Acts. Some attendees were coming to the feasts greedy for the shared food. Some were getting drunk. Some were excluding widows and various ethnicities. Like all followers of Christ, our quest to serve each other with gladness and sincerity of heart gets tested constantly, and often we fail. Satan, the deceiver, continues to work at marring our fellowship time with God and with each other. We need to be on the defensive against deceptions, and on the offensive for reaching out in love.

Hospitality in our churches needs to spring from lives sincerely touched by God before we enter the manmade structures we mistakenly confuse with God's church. We ought to be gladly welcoming others to the assembly wherever we happen to meet. The worship and communion services should be meaningful and fresh each week. The hospitality around the worship service must be intentional and meaningful. It needs to go beyond the type of coffee and tea served before or after church, (which might be worth upgrading), and the occasional potluck supper.

As Christians, loving the strangers who come to our church door starts in our own homes, and our community spaces, and continues into the sanctuaries of our churches. It can be seen in the way we offer a smile and speak kindly to those in line with us at the grocery store. It can include setting aside parking spaces for guests, good signage, and being attentive to the needs of families with young children, and the elderly. It includes being on the watch for singles who arrive alone and deserve to be welcomed, asked if they would like to sit near us, and invited to connect after services.

Just a few weeks ago, I noticed a young single man sitting alone a few seats down from me. There was another single young man sitting alone behind him. Before the service, I introduced myself to one, and then the other. They both said they had planned on meeting friends at the service. For some reason, neither of their "friends" showed up. After the service, I made a point to speak to each of them again and introduced them to each other joking how they had a lot in common having both been "ghosted" at church. They laughed and promised to come another week whether their "friends" came, or not.

Even at my age, it takes a bit of courage to reach out and to make myself a bit vulnerable, but it is always worth it.

A few weeks ago, we visited a small church in the mountains of North Carolina. They have a special ministry for the many summer visitors who come to the area from May to September. This church decided to draw people to their services by featuring great local music with fiddles, banjos, bass, violins, and other instruments. The church seats about eighty people inside. During the summer season, they put up a tent outside with chairs and loudspeakers where another eighty can sit and participate in the service. They have a welcome table out in front of the building where they encourage everyone to make a name tag to facilitate knowing and being known.

The Sunday we attended was the last one for the season and had a crowd of people who overflowed the overflow tent. As more people poured onto the grounds, the woman in charge of welcoming guests brought out blankets and even garbage bags for people to sit on in the yard. She was gracious and never stopped smiling, taking songbooks from some she had already handed them to and asking everyone to share. When it came time for communion, the minister warned us they were not prepared for such a large crowd, and he might have to break the "hosts" in half. We knew God would provide, and He did. There were dogs, kids, and lots of people having a wonderful time of communion and community!

A college campus ministry I have been part of is taking a whole year to emphasize hospitality. They have a living/learning center where they host game and movie nights, as well as smaller student-planned monthly dinners with faculty and alumni. One of the former students who arrived on campus knowing the value of hospitality initiated what came to be known as Tea-times with Tanner. Each week, he invited a group of students to share tea and conversation in his college housing space. They could return the next week only if they brought a friend who had not been there before. In this way, Tanner got to know hundreds of students on the campus. He became a catalyst for current students who have continued his outreach.

Do we all need to have deluxe coffee bars at our churches? Parking lot ministries? Tag-wearing greeters at the door? Special music ministries? Perhaps not. However, being intentional about hospitality and loving strangers along with loving the rest of the church family goes a long way toward furthering the message and reach of God's kingdom. Yes, it starts with the leaders, but each of us plays an important part. We can all work at being more intentional.

> *Part of the church's growth in the future has a lot to do with how well we love strangers and practice hospitality each day while it is still called today.*

Ask Yourself...

Do I think it should be a requirement for church leaders (ministers and elders) to practice hospitality?

_____

_____

What have I seen done well as far as church hospitality? .... Poorly?

_____

_____

When was the last time I met someone new at church? .... Invited someone to church with me? .... Invited someone to sit with me?

_____

_____

Have I offered to join a team to serve others?

_____

_____

What do I think it means to remember Christ in the "breaking of the bread"?

_____

_____

Dig Deeper:

Read Acts 2:42-47.

Is there anything new you can incorporate into your church practice?

_____

_____

_____

Read 1 Timothy 3:2 and 1 Peter 4:9-11.

Do you think practicing hospitality at churches makes a difference in growing the kingdom of God?

_____

_____

"If you really want to make a friend, go to someone's house and eat with him...
the people who give you their food give you their heart"
– Cesar Chavez[12] (sophisticatedgourmet.com)

---

[12] (sophisticatedgourmet.com)

CHAPTER 12

Breaking Bread Together

When he was at the table with them, he took bread, gave thanks, broke it and began to give it to them. Then their eyes were opened and they recognized him... (Luke 24:31 NIV)

Throughout this book, I have emphasized opening the door and inviting strangers into our own homes. Often, this has involved lots of people and sometimes overnight or longer stays. As I continue to encourage you to be open to these possibilities, I do not want to overlook the power of a simple or single shared meal.

It takes courage to remember that biblical hospitality is radically different, in purpose and preparation, than merely entertaining guests. We live in an age when the pressure of social media and other forces keep us from inviting others to simply break bread with us in our homes, or even invite them for coffee and conversation. We should not be concerned about gaining likes and hearts on Facebook, Pinterest, and Instagram. Inviting people we don't know well to a meal and authentic conversation can take us out of our comfort zones. It's personal and can make us feel vulnerable. We must ask ourselves, *Am I trying to bless or impress?*

For example, I have often been guilty of marring the sacred practice of hospitality by trying to impress rather than simply bless my guests by showing love for them. Sometimes, I spend too much time and energy trying to esthetically please my own taste, overthinking what to serve, how to coordinate napkins and placemats, or getting anxious about shopping. There are times I have found myself watching the clock and hoping guests won't arrive until I have the house and myself cleaned up and looking relatively neat.

The worst mistake is when in the haste of getting other things done, I neglect to make my heart ready to focus on the pure joy of loving my guests and preparing to be present with them. Yes, I want my guests to feel loved, but secretly hope the décor will compensate for my less-than-inspiring cooking skills, or that the store-bought desserts will not bring judgment on me.

Beautiful tables and picturesque plating of delicious food are not evil. They can enhance any shared time together and delight the eyes and stomachs of all who are invited. I have felt the love when I am treated to these things by gracious hosts. Those meals are even worthy of a picture captured on our phones. However, focusing on the stuff and not the strangers can also drain the power out of the purpose of sharing meals together.

Each day I am learning more about how to keep my motives pure and extend and accept invitations without fear or anxiety. When I remember the definition of hospitality as "loving strangers," it helps me to focus on the people and not the preparation. Surprisingly, the preparation becomes much easier.

The story of Mary and Martha found in the gospel of Luke 10:38-42 (NIV) is a beautiful illustration of biblical hospitality:

> *As Jesus and his disciples were on their way, he came to a village where a woman named Martha opened her home to him. She had a sister called Mary, who sat at the Lord's feet listening to what he said. But Martha was distracted by all the preparations that had to be made. She came to him and asked, "Lord, don't you care that my sister has left me to do the work by myself? Tell her to help me!"*

*"Martha, Martha," the Lord answered, "you are worried
and upset about many things, but few things are needed—
or indeed only one. Mary has chosen what is better, and
it will not be taken away from her."*

The narrative acknowledges it was Martha's home and she was the one who "opened her home" to Jesus and several of His disciples who were traveling with Him. Well done, Martha! It also says there were "preparations that had to be made." No disputing that fact. When we invite people in, it seems the right thing to do is to offer them food and drink, which might mean some work on our part. Martha was working hard and resentful of her sister who was not helping her. She was grumbling! She appealed to Jesus to ask Mary to help her. Instead, Jesus helps Martha in an even more life-giving way than Mary ever could have by helping with the dishes.

In His gentle yet humbling reply, Jesus reminds Martha and us, "Few things are needed, indeed only one. Mary has chosen what is better." We can imagine the tears in Martha's eyes, the flush in her face, and the sag in her tired shoulders. Hopefully, Martha felt the love in Jesus' voice as He acknowledged her worry and frustration. He gently redirected her attention from the "needed preparations" to the person who wanted to be seen and heard, Jesus himself. The reason I can imagine this scene so well is because I have felt the same gentle rebuke of the Holy Spirit who has redirected my energy to the important things.

When my focus is on my guest (stranger or friend), it changes everything. Like the travelers on the road to Emmaus, my heart feels warm when I look into the eyes of those at the table with me. The story in Luke 24:13-35 takes place shortly after Jesus has been raised from the dead. The travelers are headed out of Jerusalem. Jesus walks and talks to them explaining the scriptures concerning Himself although they don't recognize Him.

They stop at their village and invite this "stranger" who has walked with them to share a meal and stay with them. It is not until Jesus breaks bread with them that their eyes are opened, and they recognized Him. After Jesus disappears from their sight, they recall how their hearts burned within them.

Often, I feel the presence of God in a similar way because I see Him in the face and story of those created in His image whom I have the privilege of breaking bread with. This is one of the primary reasons I believe God encourages us to practice hospitality.

It doesn't have to require stress or great toil on our part. It doesn't have to impress. It does require a focus on the stranger. Looking at them, listening to them, and loving them with the love that comes from God. No one leaving my home has complained about my messy desk or the burnt garlic bread. In fact, those may be some of the reasons many have felt safe in returning for more conversation and connection. The scratches on my tables and stains on my rugs all tell stories. Good stories of furnishings used to bless others.

I recently told some friends what I was learning about hospitality, and their eyes lit up as they eagerly told me about their recent experience hosting an international student for a weekend. They were reluctant to sign up when asked by another friend, who was very involved with the international student ministry because they had never before had a stranger in their home overnight. They were shocked and delighted by how transforming the weekend was for them and this young woman from a Middle Eastern country. They felt the presence of God throughout the weekend, and a stranger became a friend. The blessing received from offering hospitality that my friend experienced is something all of us can participate in.

> *This is the day. This is the time. Let's love the strangers God brings into our lives. Let's open the door to see them, hear them, love them. Let's practice godly hospitality. You will be blessed when you do.*

Ask Yourself...

What is the difference between hospitality and entertaining?

_____

_____

Do you identify more with Mary or Martha?

_____

_____

What can you learn from the character you do not identify with?

_____

_____

Dig Deeper:

Read Luke 24:13-35

Have you ever had an experience, like those traveling to Emmaus, where your "eyes were opened" to a new knowledge or understanding of Jesus.

_____

_____

Read Hebrews 13:2

Have you ever had an experience where you came to realize that you had entertained angels?

_____

_____

Read Matthew 24: 37-40

Have you ever done something for a needy person (one of the least of these) and felt the pleasure of God?

_____

_____

Final Word

Thank you for coming with me on this journey to discover what it means to practice Biblical Hospitality. Honestly, when I started writing things down a few months ago, I had no idea that God would open my eyes to see how truly important it is that we revitalize this practice in our lives. My original intent was to capture some of the wonderful experiences as a guest and host that God has allowed me and my family to be a part of. I wanted to make sure that my grandchildren had a written record of how God has used the practice of hospitality to change our lives by allowing us to intersect with the lives of so many amazing strangers from around the world. We have also learned so much about God, his heart for strangers, and his ability to miraculously supply all our needs and the needs of others.

I hope my stories have encouraged you. I have plenty more. I have been invited to homes with dirt floors and sheets for doors in Honduran villages, and also invited to "tea and vittles" at the White House by the President. I have been the grateful recipient of genuine hospitality offered in each of those instances and many in between. Each occasion has blessed me and changed me. Those experiences have enriched my life in ways I can never repay, except perhaps by paying them forward and continuing to offer hospitality to those around me.

In a world that seems to grow increasingly hostile and fearful, loving strangers and practicing hospitality can begin to break through the fear. It can bring the light of Christ into those dark places.

Teaching the practice of hospitality to our children and grandchildren is vital. Who knows? It might be one of the keys to less bullying on school playgrounds. It might be one of the keys to "a more perfect union" in the US, even during election years! It may be one of the keys to safer neighborhoods as we reach out and connect with our neighbors one by one. It may be part of the restoration and healing needed from the damage done by a world-wide pandemic. I am certain it will be a catalyst for increased church attendance and church growth.

When we are intentional about really seeing and listening to others who are strangers to us, whether offering a smile, a hand, a seat next to us, or breaking bread together, we do it for Christ himself. When we commit to "love strangers as family" God's kingdom comes. His will is done in a special way.

Final Word

Many of you reading this book have already discovered the power and grace that comes with practicing hospitality. I want to hear your stories. **You can contact me at my email AnniesHospitalityBook@gmail.com** or my website **www.AnnieBooks.com.** If you are reading this and have yet to understand its power, I would love to hear from you too. What is holding you back? Did anything encourage you to begin this important practice? I humbly invite you to get started and join me in taking the risk. There are strangers all around us just waiting to be loved. God will help us. Hospitality is in His nature, and He has imparted that nature to us. Don't miss out on the joy and grace of loving strangers through the practice of hospitality. Let's start today.

About the Author

Annie McCune believes in God, as known through the Father, Son, and Holy Spirit. She is delighted to have discovered the continual joy of obeying His command to practice hospitality.

She grew up in a large and loving family in Western New York. She graduated from Dartmouth College where she encountered Christ as her Lord and Savior, and met her husband, Lee.

Together they have 4 children, who are married to terrific spouses with 12 amazing grandchildren. There are also 4 bonus children, their spouses, and 8 bonus grandkids you will read about in the book.

God has given her various assignments over the years including helping to organize Prayer Events that have been city-wide, state-wide, and worldwide.

Her favorite assignment, after loving God and her family, is loving the strangers God puts in her path, and having them become family and friends.

She can be contacted at AnniesHospitalityBook@ gmail.com.